...AND WHAT THE CRITICS HAVE SAID ABOUT LORENZO W. MILAM'S OTHER WRITINGS

"...he can in a moment merge the painful and the comic..."
— THE [LONDON] TIMES LITERARY SUPPLEMENT

"By turns bemused, polemical, and absurdist..."
— THE WHOLE EARTH REVIEW

"...unabashedly journalistic, highly idiosyncratic, and full of raciness, wit, and irreverence."
— THE DURHAM UNIVERSITY JOURNAL (of England)

"...excellent reading."   — JOURNALISM HISTORY

"His comments are often biting and hilarious."
— CONTEMPORARY PSYCHOLOGY

"...entertains with dark humor..."   — LIBRARY JOURNAL

"...never dull."   — MIDWEST BOOK REVIEW

CripZen
A MANUAL FOR SURVIVAL

by
Lorenzo Wilson Milam

MHO & MHO WORKS
1993
San Diego, California

Published by Mho & Mho Works.
For a complete catalogue of our other books, send a stamped self-addressed
envelope to
  Box 33135
  San Diego, California 92163
Library of Congress Cataloging-in-Publication Data:
Milam, Lorenzo W.
    CripZen : a manual for survival / by Lorenzo Wilson Milam.
      p.   cm.
    Includes index.
    ISBN 0-917320-02-6 : $17.95. — ISBN 0-917320-03-4 (pbk.) : $12.95
    1. Physically handicapped—United States—Psychology.
2. Physically handicapped—United States—Religious life.
I. Title
HV3023.A3M55   1993
155.9'16—dc20   92-27207

                                              CIP

First Edition
Cover Design by Lolita Lark
Printed in the United States of America
  2 3 4 5 6 7 8 9 10 J Q K A

CRIPZEN
A MANUAL FOR SURVIVAL

*"Some believe the word 'cripple' is a sentence
without a period..."*

— BLAISE CENDRARS

OTHER BOOKS BY LORENZO W. MILAM

Under A Bed of Poses, A Novel (1959)

The Myrkin Papers (1969)

*Sex & Broadcasting: A Handbook on Building a Station
for the Community* (1974)

The Cripple Liberation Front Marching Band Blues
(1984)

The Radio Papers (1986)

The Lourdes of Arizona, by Carlos Amantea (1989)

The Blob That Ate Oaxaca, by Carlos Amantea (1992)

CONTENTS

I. ADVICE

II. ARTICLES

III. REVIEWS

IV. CRIPZEN

V. FOUR PATHS

VI. APPENDICES

VII. THE AUTHORS

PREFACE

CripZen is a survival kit for those of us who are variously designated as "handicapped," "disabled," "other-abled," "differently-abled," or some such nonsense.

With or without a label, we know who we are. Know that when I use the word "we" or "you" in this book, I am referring to those of us who have lost the use of part or all of our bodies.

Others — those we designate as the "temporarily-abled" — may choose to read this as well. Since we are all Crips[1] in one way or another, it is well worth learning the truth of what must befall us some day, even if it hasn't already started (it has).

⧗

Many of these articles were first published during my term as disability-sexuality columnist for *Independent Living*. Others appeared in *Spinal Network*, *Social Issues & Healthcare Review*, and *The Fessenden Review*. "My Sister" was reprinted in *The Pushcart Prize, X: Best of the Small Presses*, and part of it was broadcast on National Public Radio's "All Things Considered." "Eating Head" appeared in *Mainstream* and, with slight revisions, in *The Sun*. "A Carnival of Love" appeared in *SIHR* and — in somewhat

---

[1]During the course of this book, I will use the word "Crip." It is the only word I have found over the years that contains the pith and vigor we need to describe our condition. (That is, too, why I capitalize it, like "Black" or "Jew.")

It is no accident that the most vicious of the street gangs in Los Angeles choose to call themselves "the Crips," and the meanest of them all uses the name "Water Gate Crips" after the structural disaster of the same name.

shortened form — in *The Disability Rag.* Parts of "Crip-Zen" appeared in revised form in *New Mobility.*

I must accept reluctant responsibility for the contradiction of *CripZen* — that is, that I offer a plea for Good Sex and Good Mental Health while at the same time offering a Zen model of Forget-The-Body Quiet-The-Mind.

The truth is that the hunger for love, the hunger for sanity, and the hunger for truth must feed on each other. If they cannot serve the Master, at least they can serve the Muse.

— LWM
Paradise, California
Fall, 1992

INTRODUCTION
The Second Revelation

"In one group of 59 deaths, 18 were confirmed suicides, seven were probably suicides and several others could possibly have been suicides."

A possible fifty percent suicide rate? Who *are* these people? Terminal cancer patients? The starving in Biafra? Recent widowers?

Nope. Crips. You and me.

In *Spinal Network*'s "Grim Reapings,"[2] we learn the little publicised facts about suicides of our brothers and sisters, figures drawn from a University of Alabama study. The author, Lee Slater, goes on to give us a haunting description of the deaths of two of his friends:

> *"Sam and Roger did themselves in August. That's when they do it in Florida. The heat is unrelenting, the humidity is stifling, and it rains almost every single mother-loving day. The poor ABs pick up their guns in the bad parts of town and kill each other. The quads pick up their pills and kill themselves."*

We Crips learn potent lessons about ourselves (and the world) in the early years of our new life.

First we learn that being Crip doesn't make us a better person. It may make us more understanding, or more

---

[2]"Grim Reapings: Anger Turned Inward," from the *Spinal Network Extra,* Winter, 1992.

cruel, or more astute, or more suicidal, or more cagey — but we don't become sanctified in the process.

Second, unless we're famous, our physical condition makes little difference to humanity. It may stagger us, blow away our friends and families (it may even blow them apart) — but to most mortals, it's just another in a long line of Sad Stories. The world moves on, and if we think it will respond sensibly or well (or at all) to what has happened to us, we have another think coming.

Third, we learn that our greatest enemy isn't being Crip, but, rather, what we see in the mirror. Many of us believe there is a monster staring back at us, even though our friends and would-be lovers see something completely different. Our bodies have skewed our senses, and it takes us a long time to catch up to those who have a better vision than we do.

Finally (and without a doubt the most difficult): the victories that you and I mustered up in the first few months or years of trauma were probably ersatz. Our families thought we were tremendous; our friends were inspired; even the media, in some cases, lionized us. They were all impressed with the fortitude we showed (even *we* were inspired by what they thought of as total psychic recovery).

But our great bravery, our seeming acceptance of fate, the splendid triumph of spirit over physical self — these were all put-up jobs.[3]

I say this not to be harsh on us. We had to do it; the world expected it of us and we expected it of ourselves. That we brought it off in face of such disaster might even be

---

[3]It's a western concept that we can wage a war with the body and — with sufficient determination — win. The truth is that none of us can triumph in a battle with our own mind, body, or soul. (Civil wars create waste and bitterness, not victory.)

considered miraculous. However, sooner or later, what we created out of the ashes has to give way to the real thing. "I survived, I've made a new life — but why do I feel so lousy?" is the clue.

Shrinks, as usual, have a name for it. They call it Denial. We have an answer for that one, too. Since you and I have learned such bravery, acceptance, and fortitude — we *have* to deny that we are denying. In doing that, we create something special. It's called "almost intolerable pain."

Once we come to the knowledge of the deception we have imposed on ourselves and on others, we find ourselves immersed in a new pain, and a bitter, bitter sadness. This can be fatal, as fatal as our first grief-at-loss.

⧗

I give you two articles of faith. The first is that this "Second Revelation" will come to you someday, if it hasn't already.

I also give it to you as an article of faith that when it does come, it doesn't have to kill you. Once you stumble across the truth of your being, you will find that it cannot be stolen from you. It will become part of your survival mechanism, one that even *you* won't be able to take from you. With it you can forge a powerful new system for dealing with a new world.

⧗

This is a training manual, and a survival kit. You have to do much of the work. I put it together in sequence, but you have to figure out where you are in the sequence. You have to seek out the parts that are going to be most helpful as you move along to the next stage. The only thing you cannot do is stop.

Following the commonly accepted five stages of dying, I have devised five stages leading to CripZen:

Stage I. I am not a Crip;

Stage II. I'm a Crip and I can't take it;

Stage III. I'm a Crip, but I can beat it;

Stage IV. I'm a Crip, I can beat it — but I am Still a Crip and I can't take it;

Stage V. I am that I am.[4]

How to get from I to V without going under is the subject of this book.

---

[4]See Appendix 2.

I. ADVICE

" *We can't measure spirituality in terms of what happens to us. In fact, there is no way at all to judge where we are in spiritual terms. All we can do is treat our lives, both inner and outer, with deep compassion and acceptance. Nothing else really matters.* "

— STEPHEN R. SCHWARTZ
INTERVIEW, THE SUN, *OCTOBER 1992*

GETTING A LIFE

Mr. Milam:
RE: Your article in Hippocrates *Magazine.*

> *Your attitude stinks. So you're a little bit crippled. It's up to you to put others at ease!!*
> *My son is a quad since 1986. His sense of humor has never faltered. His friends are steady. He owns and works in a sporting goods store. He works with the public everyday and doesn't have your "Poor-Me" attitude.*
> *Get a life.*

> *E.L.H*
> *Dallas TX*

Dear Mr. H:

THANK YOU FOR YOUR POST-CARD OF 8 November.

The article that appeared in *Hippocrates* was from my autobiography, *The Cripple Liberation Front Marching Band Blues.* It was a small (two-page) excerpt out of a fairly extensive book on what it means to be disabled.

My book was written as an antidote to the Life-Is-Great-No-Matter-What-Happens message that has plagued us since the advent of the good Dr. Norman Vincent Peale.

The book does indeed contain self-pity, despair, and anger. It also contains hope, joy, love, and finally an epiphany (of sorts). It was praised in several dozen magazines and newspapers, including *Newsday,* the *Los Angeles*

Herald-Examiner, and the august *Journal of the American Medical Association*.

The book was an attempt to show what the newly disabled go through, steps that are very similar to Kubler-Ross's five stages: anger, self-pity, depression, bargaining, and acceptance. I suspect the excerpt was chosen by *Hippocrites* as an example of the anger and distancing that occurs when we lose a part of our body — something well known to medical professionals, but which is, all too often, hidden from family and friends.

There are days when your son feels sharp, bright, alive, conquering, in control, full of optimism and joy. These times he no doubt shares with you.

But then you say, "His sense of humor has never faltered…He works with the public every day and doesn't have a 'poor-me' attitude."

From my more than thirty-five years of experience, I would suggest to you that there are times when his humor falters. There are days when, I suspect, he feels despair, angst, the blues. There are days, most probably, when he wouldn't reveal to you or anyone else his real grief at his all-too-human situation. He keeps it inside. Many of us have to because there is an unspoken demand by the world that those dark thoughts be hidden away.

I've never met you, but from having read your crisp condemnation of me, I have to tell you that I know you well. You are one of the legions who tell us what we *should* feel, as opposed to what we *do* feel. We have met you thousands of times before, and you drive us up the wall.

I would guess your deepest fear is that your son is, after all these years, still capable of grieving over his loss-of-body. Your fear — perhaps his too — is that if he would ever let the truth out, even for a moment, the two of you would lose something very important, like your silver-lined world. It is all part of denial, and it can be a malicious double-bind for all of us. It tells us that when we are in the dumps and show it, we are being Bad, as in Bad Boy, or Bad Cripple.

I tell you all this not to make you more angry or troubled than you already are. God knows I know that the accident of seven years ago has deeply scarred the two of you, and probably others. Your son knows — intimately — loss-of-body; he's even seen some of society's more debilitating ways of dealing with it. It is, in the cruellest sense, the gift that keeps on giving.

You can't make your son's life more worthy by demanding that he hide from his pain. It is real and it is there, and it will be expressed, either directly or indirectly, today, tomorrow, next year, ten years from now — whether you wish it or no. There are a multitude of ways it might surface. Bitterness and anger are the most common and recognizable. Less obvious, but as hurtful, is what we call the Roosevelt Syndrome — scaling great heights, smiling, waving to the crowd, becoming SuperCrip, convincing everyone that there is nothing going on inside, nothing at all.

To many it seems to be the Best Way, but in truth, as Hugh Gallagher has shown in his book *FDR's Splendid Deception*, the price for denial for all (family, friends, the disabled person him- or herself) is grievous indeed.[1]

I assure you I don't want to come on to you and your world like some dark cloud. There are times when we feel

---

[1] See the review of this book at the end of Section III.

great, sometimes despite our bodies, sometimes *because of* our bodies. After all, we fight a dozen small battles daily — curbs, unyielding doors, unyielding people, loneliness — and our triumphs can be real and glorious.

But what leads many of us into despair is the suspicion that we have to smile bravely at all times, every day, so the world will believe we are not depressed, or grieving. As one of my friends says with characteristic understatement, "Being disabled is no piece of cake."

I urge you to recognize the truth of the heart of us: that sometimes we are sad, sometimes joyful, but never ever "never faltering." That is a contradiction of what it means to be alive, and there are times when grief must out; as must, ultimately, our acceptance of what we are.

It is very significant that your son didn't write me and say "Your attitude stinks...Get a life."

He knows better.

Lorenzo W. Milam

THE WHORES COME IN CANDY-STRIPE BUSES

THERE IS A GRAND BOOK I READ twenty years ago. It was by a sex therapist from Scandinavia. She was writing about what she called "the sexual minorities." She said that the greatest sexual minorities are the permanently disabled, especially those who are in hospitals and nursing homes. She said that the ethics of these places dictate that we should have no sexual freedom whatsoever: no love, no passion, no exit.

People locked in such warehouses are doing double duty. Society suppresses sex for the obvious reasons: because it is so embarrassing, the power of it is so incomprehensible. (Like religion, and money — the whole question of sex creates such a tangled web of fear.)

Sex and the disabled? It's doubly fraught. The disabled are not supposed to think of, want, need, be able to have sex. It is a contradiction in terms, and in comprehension. We've become society's eunuchs.

But (as one of my favorite writers said) we dam sexuality at our own risk. It can be channeled and redirected — but when we try to block its force totally, we create monsters, both within and without.

I see quadriplegics, MS'ers, old polios, the blind, heart-attack victims, putting their sexuality on the back burner, or, worse, trying to snuff the flames entirely. Sexuality thus ceases to be a problem (they think). Lack of sexuality becomes a preference, right?

And then I remember this wonderful book from Sweden about sexual minorities. The doctor who wrote it wanted to set up these buses, these CIRCUS buses. And what would they be carrying around? Whores!

The prostitutes would be bussed into the big hospitals. You know them, you know them well — those drab dark hospitals and nursing homes, with their drab olive-green walls, and their smells — the smells of decay and sadness and dried-up grief. We've all known places like that.

The whores would come in, a dozen of them, fifteen, two dozen. Each would be assigned a patient, or two — to love, to give love to, to hold. The first time in a long time, for some of of the patients (I almost wrote prisoners.) For some of them, the first time — ever.

And for those who couldn't get it up? Or for those who had no feeling down there? Manipulation, visual stimulus, words, words whispered in the ears; hands stimulating any part of the body, any part where the feelings of love had been transferred. (And they have moved somewhere; they always do: to the neck, the earlobes, the lips, the shoulders; the armpits: they say that's one of the most sensuous parts of the body.) The hands everywhere — and sweet whispers.

A carnival of love. Every month, the red-and-white striped, yellow-wheeled busses would pull up to the nursing homes in the city: the "chronics," the "patients" given great gouts of love, from professionals.

Would the nurses be scandalized? Of course. The politicians? Horrified! The establishment? The editorials would fly. Did you hear what they were doing at the Vets' hospital? They are letting the — (what do they call them?) the "chronics:" they are letting them have whores on the wards! Can you believe it? Whores getting paid with tax-payers' money.

And everyone would be appalled, outraged, trying to stop it…this, this…going on in our warehouses, for the Permanently Disabled. Everyone…everyone…except Charlie.

Charlie has been there at the Veteran's Home for twenty — no, let's see, it's twenty-two years now. He just lies there, watching television, smoking cigarettes. The orderlies feed him, clean him up. He has no family — no one who comes to see him. There was an uncle, back, when? 1970? 1972? The old fellow finally died or just went away, was never seen again.

Charlie sometimes thinks on the days, back then, when he was eighteen, before he (or anyone) ever heard of Viet Nam. Him so young, full of piss and vinegar — going out with his girl, Janine, and sometimes late at night, she would hold him, in the front of the old coupe (a '59 Plymouth, tan, with fender skirts) she would hold him, hold him so tight, and it was like he was going to burst, the feel of her soft hair on his face, that wonderful aroma — what was it? — the smell of woman. And they would be so close that he thought he was going to burst…

…that was before Viet Nam, and the land mines. They had told him about the mines, but he never guessed, never ever guessed what a land mine could do to the body, to the legs, to the gentle parts of him down there, to the soul. He had never guessed. We kids were so innocent, so very innocent…

And since then…what has it been?…since 1965 — over two decades, Charlie has been, first, in the Veteran's hospital (two and a half years, twelve operations; not many of them successful). And then here in the nursing home. His family? They've just died off. Like his friends. Died off, or disappeared. Now there are the orderlies, and the aides, and the other patients… and the tv…

The sound of shooting — rockets, and the bombs, on tv, it still jolts him some when he hears it. The noises of war, on tv, and the noises of the ward, the dinner trays coming up. Sometimes he eats — but mostly he just lies there, smoking Camels. And there's no one except the nurses to remind him of Janine, and the time two decades ago…

⧗

Everyone thinks the "Whore Bus" is a scandal. Everyone in town. Except Charlie — and a few of his buddies on the ward. Because there is something he hasn't known for twenty years. The touch of a woman…watching her as she comes close to him. Her hands. Her hair falling down just SO…

It's been twenty years. "My God," he thinks: "How beautiful…her hands, and her eyes. For me…"

Everyone's against it. Except Charlie…and a few of his buddies, there on the ward…

THE FETISH-OF-THE-WEEK CLUB

FETISH…3. Psychol. *any object, part of the body, etc., that, although not of a sexual nature, causes an erotic response or fixation.*

"Fetishists," she said. "You have to watch out for Fetishists."

"Fascists?" I said.

"No — 'Fetishists.' I can't stand them."

"How do you recognize them?" I asked.

"You'll know, you'll know…" You'll know, she said, about these fetishists — but I was not so sure that I did. Or if I did, I wasn't so sure I understood.

THE CLASSIC BOOK ON FETISHES IS *Psychopathia Sexualis* by the British psychologist Havelock Ellis. I remember it well. It was one of those clinical, supposedly lewd books I used to borrow from my dad's locked liquor closet whenever he went out of town. Socks, shoes, gloves? I remember those, detailed "case studies" with numbers and initials. "Case #44. B. D. *Fixation on Women's Hats.*" Or stockings. Or panties. But fixation on disabled women? I didn't remember that one.

Lisa is the one who told me about it. Lisa is thirty-eight, Multiple Sclerosis, degree in MFCC (marriage, family, and child counselling), in practice for a dozen or so years, working mostly with disabled women. She had been referred to me as a good source of knowledge and wisdom on love, and women, and disability.

"In my women's group," Lisa tells me, "every one of us, without exception, has met men who were interested in us, men who seemed perfect to date, as potential lovers, and then — you find out that they aren't interested in you. They are *very* interested in your disability, and your helplessness.

"We're all hungry for love," says Lisa. "For disabled women, it can be a desperate seeking. And here, at last, someone comes down the pike who seems perfect. Someone who wants to be with us, to spend time with us, seems to find us sexy....and then..."

"And then?..."

"You have to get away from them. They want to own you. It's power. It's not love..."

"Are you sure about that?" I say. "Are they really harmful?" I have my doubts. "Isn't it possible," I wonder, "that all of us have this controlling element in us? And that these characters just have it in high relief? Does it have to be destructive?" I think of the story about these guys who have this *thing* about women's feet, and how they make the greatest shoe salesmen. Or about the masochist who says to the sadist, "Beat me." And the sadist says, "No."

"You're a man," she says. "It might not be the same thing for you. It has to do with control and escape. Some of us can't escape. We can't get out of the house, out of the room. Some of us can't even get out of bed. And our bodies — we certainly can't get out of our bodies..."

"Wait a minute," I want to say: "You and your clients are not the only ones. There are others of us who can't escape." But it sets me to thinking. I remember something Rachael (my friend, and my shrink) told me, so long ago. About these three-hundred pound women ending up with men, these abusive men. The message was,

"You're fat. You should be grateful that you have me. Who else would have you?" And when the women struggled to break the pattern, go on a diet, find a therapist — it would be their men who interfered. "They would be the ones who started bringing home the cake and ice-cream," Rachael said, "to keep them in prison in their bodies.

"It's a mutual pathology," Rachael told me. "If you have a lousy self-image, the image of being a helpless cripple — for example — someone will come along to agree with that projection." To fill the hole, to complete the gestalt.

"How do we know it's happening?" I asked.

"You'll know," she said, "you'll know." Something is missing. The relationship is closed off, sealed, suffocating. "Your friends are driven away (or drift away). You find yourself feeling trapped, but thinking, 'This is all I deserve.' This creep makes you think he is doing you a great favor by being there. If you ever find yourself saying, 'He's so much more than I deserve,' then you're in one of those relationships. A healthy relationship is complementary — sometimes you're up, sometimes you're down. In this one you're always down. He owns you."

"You might know what I am talking about," says Lisa. "These *fetishist* relationships. I think men have them as well." I find myself remembering a time, so long ago, there was this woman, and she seemed so interested in me. Almost too interested, if such was possible (how could anyone have been *too* interested in me, in the state I was in

at age twenty, just out of the hospital, seeing myself —
always seeing myself — as so very ugly?)

It was something more than love, or passion. It was
this feeling I had when I was with her — like she was a
great big bird, closing in on me, trying to smother me with
her wings. I had this strange feeling that there was no way
out, no way for me to get away from her.

"I think I know what you are talking about," I say.
"It has to do with how we feel about ourselves."

"It has to do with self-love, self-esteem, self-
respect," Lisa says. "And sometimes even those aren't strong
enough to protect us. We think of ourselves as being
unsexy, unloveable, unloved. We're very vulnerable, and
these people find us — God knows how. We think they're
special, sent to help us out of the hole. But they want
something else from us. They want to use us every way they
can — physically, sexually, emotionally. They want to plant
themselves in among our weaknesses. Does that make any
sense?"

"Yeah," I say, remembering the way this woman
would look at me, as if she wanted something, something
more than I could ever possibly give her. "I know exactly
what you are talking about," I say.

LOVE WITH
A SEX-SURROGATE

THE GREAT PROBLEM IS NOT DESIRE. The great problem is manifesting that desire — despite all our fears and tremblings.

To have the passion is one thing; the dream of acting it out can be simple. The final step is always the clinker. It's the dividing line that catches us — what T. S. Eliot called the Shadow between thought and deed,

> *Between the idea*
> *And the reality*
> *Between the motion*
> *And the act*
> *Falls the Shadow...*

You and I may be hurting. We may be torn by desire — yet to find someone who can help us is (we think) impossible. The pain comes in letting others know that we are lonely and hurting. Picking up the telephone, placing the ad, exposing ourselves — all these become monumental.

With the blocking comes fear, a fear so powerful that some of us never make it across the shadowline.

Mark O'Brien is thirty-six years old. He had polio three decades ago. He lives by himself in a apartment in Berkeley, and spends most of his time in an iron lung. He writes that he learned about sex when he was seventeen:

> *Though I couldn't use my hands, I used a dirty mind and my left leg, which I can lift a bit. I would lift the leg and drop it on my genitals, all the while pretending*

someone was hurting me. Well, someone was. Me. Since then, I've associated horniness with pain and humiliation.

Like many of us, Mark was taught that sexuality was a dirty secret. He was taught, too, that for those of us with imperfect bodies, passion was shameful:

I felt ashamed of and embarrassed by my sexuality. It seemed to be utterly without any purpose in my life, except to mortify me during bedbaths. Whenever I became aroused in these situations, I wanted to die. I would not talk about my bedbath orgasms or the blazing shame I felt to my attendants, feeling that they already hated me and that talking about these matters would only intensify their fury at me. I hated being sexual.

One day, unlike many of us, Mark decided to do something about it. He told his psychotherapist that he wanted to meet a sex surrogate. A sex surrogate is a person who will, for a fee, participate in sex with a client. In most states, they can be referred only by licensed therapists.

The job of sex surrogates is to help those of us who, because of fear, shyness, or disability (emotional or physical) are incapable of participating in sexual experience in the "normal" way, e.g., through the typical societal maze set up for the satisfaction of desire: dates, the finding of mates, love.

Surrogates claim that merely having sex with a client isn't what they are about. They are trained in the facts of psychology and the physiology of sex. Being professionals in a very controversial field (filled as it is with all sorts of amateurs), they help people resolve serious sexual dysfunctions. Their task is to use a professional status to help people out of insoluable binds.

Mark's reasoning was simple and direct: he was almost forty, had never had intimacy in any way with any person, and noticed that he had started to use a variety of excuses to keep himself away from any sexual experience. With startling honesty, he outlines some of these excuses:

> *I rationalized that someone who was not an attendant, nurse, or doctor would freak out upon seeing my pale, thin body with its bent spine, bent neck, washboard ribcage, and hipbones protruding like outriggers...*

His body — or the imagined lacks in his body — was one thing; the stuff in his head was another:

> *It was not an easy decision for me. What would my parents think? What would my friends think? What would God think? I still suspected that my parents would know if I saw a surrogate, perhaps before God did.*

Overcoming a dozen problems (real and imagined), Mark finally arranged to meet with the sex therapist. He describes precisely the care with which he and his friends arranged date, time and setting. The day arrives, the therapist arrives, and after a brief conversation, she asks if she can undress him:

> *My heart pounded as fast as it ever had as she kneeled on the bed and unbuttoned my red shirt. It wasn't lust, it was pure terror that got my heart pumping so hard. She had trouble undressing me, never having done it before.*

I felt awkward and wondered if she would change her mind and leave once she saw me naked...

A rich description, this. That fear — that terrible soulripping fear that so many of us have: *once they see me without my clothes, once they see how grotesque I am — they'll be heading out the door.* Our fears working overtime to keep us separate, and alone, out of touch with ourselves, with the world.

The rest of Mark's story is one of experimentation, real passion, fruition, and completion — but it is not merely a physical completion. After the surrogate has gone, his attendant returns, and she asks what happened:

I told her it had been great, that this experience had changed my life. I felt victorious, cleansed, relieved. I had done something that I had feared and I had enjoyed it. Nothing had gone wrong. As my attendant dressed me, she congratulated me in a caring way, knowing how difficult it had been for me to decide to see a surrogate.

Is it right to speak of an orgasm as cleansing, especially when one has waited, waited so long, waited and believed for so long that the reality of it was out of one's grasp?

My sexual desires, which I had never ever talked about much, were now recognized and approved by society (or everyone I know, which felt like the same thing). Now it would be easier for me to accept my sexual desires. For the first time, I felt glad to be male, adult, and sexual.

Again, as T. S. Eliot wrote, in the *Four Quartets*,
Footfalls echo in the memory
Down the passage which we did not take
Towards the door we never opened
Into the-rose garden. My words echo
Thus, in your mind.

ADDENDUM

The Illinois Department of Rehabilitation Services has recently put out a special issue of its quarterly, entitled "Sexuality and Disability." It has generated no little foofaraw in the national press: articles of the "out of the dark closet" and "now it can be told" variety. The booklet is, however, pretty tame stuff. There's an interview with Dr. Mark Elliott of the Masters and Johnson Institute, with lots of careful and clinical ho-hum answers to the usual careful and clinical ho-hum questions. There is a list of twenty-one books, including some on fairly specific topics (*Sexuality and Multiple Sclerosis*; *Sex Education for Deaf-Blind Students*.) There's a reprint from *The Sensuous Wheeler*[2] about how counselors can best respond to hard questions we might lay on them (including some fairly dopey samples — Q: "People who talk about sex are perverted." — A: *Wrong*...)

Then there's an article by Ellen Stohl. You remember her. She's the spinal-injured lady who modelled for *Playboy*. Her model job quite stirred up the pot: there was some discussion about exploitation and all that. However, what she has to say here is pretty clear and direct — even dramatic — and it alone might make it worthwhile for you to order the brochure. It's free from the office of Media and Public Affairs, Box 19429, Springfield IL 62794.

---

[2]*Sexual Adjustment for the Spinal Cord Injured*, by Barry Rabin.

MASTURBATION AND SELF LOVE

WE LIVE IN A CONSUMERIST SOCI-
ety. Not Communist, not Capitalist — but
Consumerist (we are all consumers.)

One of the difficulties of the Consumerist society is that our images of ourselves are shaped not by the truth, not even by fiction — but that half-truth/half-fiction called "advertising."

In this strange world, the following facts hold true:

1) We're all young;

2) And happy;

3) (Or at least fun-loving).

4) Those who aren't young and happy (and fun-loving) don't exist.

It's a simple world out there in Advertising Land — and you and I are affected by it a thousand times a day. For not only does it present us with a skewed view of the world, it distorts and tarnishes our own self-image. In fact, it tells us that some of us don't exist at all.

For most television viewers, the 45,000,000 disabled in this country don't exist, nor do our problems exist. TV shows our strengths from time to time, but our weaknesses, our moods, our tragedies — our *humanness* — are nowhere to be found. We are the Invisible Minority.

One of the themes of this column has been that delusions can be very hurtful. Being disabled is a devastating experience, and the feelings of those of us who have lived through it are potent. For some of us, at some time in our lives, these feelings have turned to poison. This poison often moves inwards on the self, with concurrent depression, sulking, murderous moods, and a foul self-image.

Self-hate and a wretched self-image can lead to a wretched life. If you and I look in the mirror and don't like what we see, we carry a double burden around with us. Not only do we have to deal with the reality ("I'm in a wheel-chair"), we have to deal with the add-on, a weighty footnote to our presumed reality — ("I'm in a wheel-chair and I'm *really* ugly.")

Some of the suggestions I've made in these columns have to do with getting ourselves away from this repressive self-image. The first step — a key step — is to begin changing the way we practice our sexuality. Options include massage, physical experimentation, opening the mind, dropping prejudices, surmounting fears — and beginning to love one's own body.

⧗

Alfred Kinsey showed that masturbation is more than a joke — although it is still the subject of a thousand sordid witticisms ("Stop the bus and let my friend Jack off"). Kinsey also proved that masturbation had a far wider clientele than anyone would have ever suspected.

He found, for example, that ninety-four percent of all males had masturbated at some time in their lives. For women, the figure is lower but, typically, more experiment with it as they get older (by the age of sixty, almost two-thirds of women have tried onanism.)

There are several books available on the subject. The most widely circulated is called *Liberating Masturbation* by Betty Dodson. My favorite, however, is *Masturba-*

tion, Tantra and Self-Love, by Margo Woods.[3] The value of it, I believe, is that it moves masturbation from the arena of "pleasure" or "necessary relief" to the arena of a spiritual experience. If one follows certain guidelines — it can be used to build a worthwhile self-image.

Ms. Woods states that one should embark on the process of self love with the same care and warmth as an assignation with a lover: oils, candles, music, a warm and scented bath. As one begins to love the body, one turns the attention from the sense organs to the heart. "The only thing to remember is that it is extremely simple," she says: one must "raise the body's sexual energy almost to the point of orgasm, and instead of letting the energy go out into the orgasm, allow it to come up in the body, up to the heart."

This system of love is derived from Indian tantric rites which include, for heterosexual love, climaxes delayed not for seconds or for minutes, but for days and weeks. Using this as her starting point, Ms. Woods suggests that we bring ourselves to the highest and closest possible point of pleasure — then stop cold, letting the kettle simmer, as it were. Then, with the mind and the breath, one places all one's attention on the heart.

Silly? Faddish? Unbearable? The reader is advised to read the book and give it a try before condemning it. Indeed, a writer for the *Spiritual Women's Times* wrote recently, "I'd like to distribute this little book to everyone because I honestly believe it has the power to transform the planet. I'm not kidding... (It) has transformed my sexuality more than any other single book."

---

[3]It is available for $9.95 + $2.00 postage from Mho & Mho Works, Box 33135, San Diego, CA 92163 [editor's note].

We can snigger whenever the subject of masturbation is brought up. But there is a chance that it might be a new way of learning to love "the me that is in me." For the 45,000,000 of us who are seen by others (and occasionally by ourselves) as outside, beyond, or below sex, *Masturbation, Tantra and Self-Love* could provide the magic we need to begin to love ourselves as we would hope to be loved by others.

CELIBACY

"As I look back upon the twenty years of the vow [of celibacy], I am filled with pleasure and wonderment. The more or less successful practice of self-control had been going on since 1901. But the freedom and joy that came to me after taking the vow had never been experienced before 1906. Before the vow I had been open to being overcome by temptation at any moment. Now the vow was a sure shield against temptation."

— *AUTOBIOGRAPHY*
MAHATMA GANDHI

"The real secret of [Roosevelt's] sex life was, probably, that there was no sex life..."

— GARRY WILLS
THE NEW YORK REVIEW OF BOOKS

ONCE, ONE OF MY MANY SHRINKS amazed me by telling me that she had given up sex some ten years before I met her. She was living with a woman she obviously cared for, but the two of them had consciously decided that their love would be enhanced if they stayed away from the whole realm of passion. Cuddling, warmth, tenderness, affection were encouraged. Lust, sex, *the beast*: no.

I have thought of her confession (to me!) a great deal since then. Like most, I have found the pursuit of sex to be satisfying (on occasion), unsatisfying (on occasion) — and almost always disruptive, often turning what could be a good friendship into a struggle of wills, a battlefield where my desires are pitched against the desires of someone I think I love.

From time to time, I have toyed with the notion of taking a hiatus from the passion game — to go celibate for a while, to debunk my idea that sex is essential for life and life essential for sex. It would not be an easy path to follow. American society drips in sensuality: it's blared at us from the advertising media, talk shows, films, videos, and magazines.

For those of us who are disabled, abandoning passion could, I suspect, be extra rewarding. Perhaps for the first time, it would give us another option. Because we can chase love and succeed, or we can chase love and fail; but we have a third choice: the choice of pursuing — willingly, gladly — a policy of no-passion.

One of the payoffs, I believe, would be the proof that we can do it — to prove that our bodies do not run us; to show the world that we have a viable alternative to mere orgasm.

⧗

Much of the inspiration for celibacy comes from the Far East. Henry C. Lea in *The History of Sacerdotal Celibacy in the Christian Church* tells us that the concept of it was common enough during Jesus's time, especially with the Essenes, who disavowed all possessions and all passion. It has been suggested that Jesus' brother James of Jerusalem was an Essene; certainly that John the Baptist was; it is even suspected that Jesus himself was. Lea states that the sect got its inspiration for self-denial from the Buddhists of India.

The Essenes, the Buddhists, and the later Catholic clergy didn't have a corner on celibacy. Though Muslims (like Jews) see procreation as "the first command," prophets of Sufism have encouraged celibacy: "There is no flame of lust that cannot be extinguished by strenuous effort because whatever vice proceeds from your self, you possess the instrument that will remove it," wrote the scholar Hujwiri. Vivekananda, the chief exponent of modern Hinduism, stated that, "in all the religious orders in the world which have produced spiritual giants you will always find absolute chastity insisted upon. That is why the monks came into existence, giving up marriage. There must be perfect chastity in thought, word, and deed…"

What does all this mean to you and to me? Perhaps one of the most unfortunate things to befall Westerners who contemplate celibacy is the belief that it must flow solely from religious belief. Celibates are monks, nuns, and thin mendicants off there in the hills somewhere. Thus, it becomes a discipline that is not available to those of us without fervent religious conviction.

Despite this, I would guess is that celibacy is practiced widely and without comment by a large segment of our population — and by largely non-religious folk. Kinsey's classic studies of sexuality in America pointed out that 1.8% - 2.1% of the total population of the United States had "no sources of outlet" e.g., no sexual relief (he was speaking about people from adolescence to age eighty-five). It doesn't sound like too many people until you multiply it out — some 4,000,000 individuals. And this four million figure is heavily skewed to the downside because Kinsey excluded those who reported nocturnal emissions (involuntary orgasms), which were experienced by another five percent of total respondents.

It all points to the existence of a fair number of practicing celibates. There are — for example — women who have willingly chosen to abandon sex and sensuality because of the possibility of disease. Then there are those who have a strong distaste for birth control methods, or — like my shrink — those who merely want to avoid the weariness that comes from the pursuit of sex. There are men that practice continency not because they are priests or monks or Sufis or Hindus, but because of weariness at the pursuit, distaste for the games, and — as compelling — the fear of AIDS.

It has been proved, despite the intervening years, and the so-called "sexual revolution," that Kinsey's figures are remarkably durable, not having changed much from when *Sexual Behavior in the Human Male* was first published. Thus, when we read that by age sixty, seven percent of married males "are no longer active," (for women the figure is closer to twenty percent) we realize that many older folks, married for decades, have quietly decided to dump passion for something more rewarding.

Nearer to home, you and I know some of our disabled brothers and sisters who practice celibacy out of apathy, timidity, repugnance, or concern at the physical effort involved. The rub, and the pity of it, is that some of us feel guilty and out-of-step because we can't find a sexual partner (perhaps we are too traumatized to even try.) We feel miserable because we think we are missing out on all the fireworks.

The key to what I am suggesting here is that the fireworks can be shot off in another direction. Celibacy can be a viable alternative to the endlessly repeated patterns of lousy courtships, frustration in relationships, ruinous impulses, and tedium in the bedroom — those ghastly experiences that lead nowhere and teach us nothing.

⌛

If one elects to become celibate — how is one to go about it? The experts tell us that diet, or, better, abandonment of certain foods, is vital. "All the other senses will automatically come under control when the palate has been brought under control," said Vivekananda. "So overpowering are the senses that they can be kept under control only when they are completely hedged in on all sides, from above and from beneath. It is common knowledge that they are powerless without food, and so fasting undertaken with a view to control of the senses is, I have no doubt, very helpful." Vivekananda and Gandhi both stated that a meatless diet is essential, meat being known to inflame the senses. (Many of us who depend on others to to help us in going to the bathroom might well have another reason to go meatless: it is a known fact that beef, pork, and other meats create the foulest smelling feces. By going vegetarian, you can render the process less distasteful for those who care for you or clean up you or your bedpan. And despite some propaganda to the contrary — careful vegetarians can get all the nutrients they need to be healthy.)

Clothing, occupation, choice of reading matter, and support from family and friends are key elements to becoming celibate. The essential factor is discipline: discipline of thought, control over "the monkey-mind."

Thoughts of passion may enter the brain, but are not allowed to tyrannize it.

By accessing the stillness within, reaching the famous Silent Mind — "the bell ringing in the empty sky" as one mystic calls it — one can create the perfect environment for freedom from the power of lust.

REFERENCES

Gandhi: A Study in Revolution, by Geoffrey Ashe. Wm. Hinemann, Ltd (1968)

Autobiography, by Mohandas K. Gandhi. Dover. (1978)

Sexual Behavior in the Human Male, Sexual Behavior in the Human Female. Alfred Kinsey, ed. W. B. Saunders (1948, 1953)

The History of Sacerdotal Celibacy in the Christian Church by Henry C. Lea. Oxford University Press (1966)

The Complete Works of Swami Vivekananda. Advaita Ashrama (1989)

GAY LOVE

Dear Mr. Milam,

My name is Phil and I have severe cerebral palsy. I am thirty-one, and completely helpless, except for typing with my head.

I am very sexually frustrated. I have no problem getting my penis fully erected. Since I was thirteen I have been masturbating by laying on my stomach and rubbing myself on the bed or floor. Now that I am thirty-one it is getting harder for me to move myself enough to cum. I really like to cum especially in hot wheather. Is there a device that I could buy that would help me to masturbate?

I really like to have my hairy anis rubbed. How can I get a man to do it? I really would like a hairy chest. Is there anyway that I can stimulate the hair to grow on my chest?

Any information that you can give me on these subjects, would be appreciated greatly.

Thank you for your time and patience, and I hope to hear from you soon.

Sincerely,
Phil
Indiana

Dear Phil:

U NLIKE MANY OF MY GENERATION, I
feel that love-for-money is not a sin, does not
have to degrade a relationship, and is — as a
matter of truth — the operating system of so many "normal" social relationships. Indeed, there are some eminent
sociologists who have pointed out that marriage is an
economic contract, perhaps even a form of classic inden-
ture. Up until the invention of "Romantic Love," marriage
was seen as an excellent way of binding two fortunes or two
political entities together. And we cling to this medieval
system, because in this most civilized of countries, a wife's
refusal to have sex with her husband is a legal basis for
ending financial support, and dissolving the marriage.

I bring up the possibility of renting love because
there are many of us who, for better or worse, don't exactly
think of ourselves as making it in the Body Beautiful
Sweepstakes — especially on the heels of some catastrophic
accident or disease. Our passion continues to work in a
normal way: it's just that the standard ways of finding love
and lovers are, we believe, impossible.

The courtship/seduction routine (dances, bowling,
dating) are — for whatever reasons — too difficult for us.
We feel degraded participating in such rituals, and yet our
lust is real and our desire to touch, to be held, is as potent, is
perhaps more potent, than before.

Several states have licensed "sex therapists." These
are men (or women) who for a fee will give love to those of
us willing to pay for it as a psychotherapeutic tool. Since the
practice is not widespread, you might be more successful in
pursuing other routes to fulfilled passion. To find heterosexual lovers-for-a-fee, one has to go no further than the

Yellow Pages. In my area, the "MASSAGE" section runs ten pages, leaving little to the imagination (*Oriental #1 Massage: Japanese Body Shampoo. Feather Touch. Very Private Rooms & Soft Music.* All this is accompanied by a picture of an Oriental-looking lady with face of ill-disguised bliss.)

Those looking for gay love may have to go further afield. You might consider subscribing to a gay publication in the nearest large city, and utilizing its "personal" ads. "The Standard Periodical Directory" — available in the public library — lists under "Homosexual Literature" more than 100 gay publications (including those with such fetching titles as "Mom...Guess What!", "Big Apple Dyke News," "Fag Rag," and "Mom's Apple Pie.") One or two of these encompass your region. I especially recommend the *Gayellow Pages* at Box 292, Village Station, New York City 10014. For $10 postpaid, they will send you a listing of switchboards and hotlines around the country, including national and regional disabled gay support groups.

There are also companies that specialize in "sex toys for the handicapped." One I have read about is called Xandria; it operates out of Box 31039, San Francisco CA 94131, advertisomg *Sexual Aids: How to order them without embarrassment. How to use them without disappointment.* The catalogue goes for $4.

⧗

I have always claimed that we Crips are doubly penalized. We live in a society in which sexuality is still taboo. The coming of AIDS has precipitated another taboo, for we now have the situation where sexual pleasure can lead to desperate sickness, and death. (This tragedy is neither novel nor new: the penalty for incautious sex was as heavy for our ancestors as it is now. For over four hundred years, until the discovery of penicillin during WWII, contracting syphilis meant a slow, lingering death — often ending in madness.)

There is another moral stricture that you and I have to deal with. It is the unspoken rule that we disabled are not to have sex — or if we do, we're not supposed to enjoy it. And if we happen to desire homosexual, lesbian, or transvestite partners — so much the worse.

These social taboos are virulent and pernicious. Equally so are the ones that live in our heads. If I do not see myself as a whole person, how can I possibly compete in the Sexuality Sweepstakes? Should I even try? It is a devilish hand that our body and society has dealt us, and it is rendered more devilish by our own feeling of wretched self-esteem. We look in the mirror, and what we see looking back at us says "Forget it!" "Who wants to make love to *that?*" we find ourselves thinking. That's the tragedy.

⧖

There is a way out — and the ball is in your court. It has to do with belief in Self, the faith that you can be loved. It has to do with vitiating the conviction, so obvious in your letter, that no-one wants you.

You are very specific in what you desire. It would be glib of me to tell you that to go for it will be easy. You already have a dozen voices in your head telling you not to do it, not to try — that if you persist, you will probably be humiliated. "Just give up and become celibate," those voices say. "Why bother?"

But to paraphrase one of my favorite bumper-stickers, *Crips Need Love Too*. You will be hurting yourself if you let shame, fear, and self-destructive attitudes keep you tied down. It might help you if I tell you about Friend Larry, who lives in a small suburb outside Detroit. After fretting for six months, he finally placed an ad in a local gay newspaper:

Help the handicapped! Severely disabled fifty-three-year-old wants male lover. Telephone XXX-XXXX.

Truth in advertising always works best. A non-specific illness had left Larry only the use of the right side of his body. He was, at least by society's lights, "severely disabled." The ad was honest. Perhaps that is why it brought in over twenty calls. After evaluating the callers, Larry met with (and interviewed) three of the most promising. Imagine having over twenty people go to so much trouble to be with you.

The ad did two things. Larry found a lover, but he gave up something in the process. He got rid of some of that shame and fear that all of us have, the voice that keeps babbling in our heads, "You're never going to find a lover. Don't even try." Larry had to short-circuit that voice to place the ad; now he scarcely hears it any more.

It isn't foolproof. But there are people out there, I'm convinced, who — for a variety of reasons — see us as desirable, and they are not necessarily the 'fetishists' I described before. There are people out there who find our bodies to be attractive — if not interesting. Larry's newest lover can't get over how his pretzel-like legs — they had been so thoroughly stretched in therapy — could be bent hither and yon. "Fascinating," he keeps saying, moving Larry's body about for him, gently.

Give it a try. It's scary. But, without love, what you are going through now may be even more scary.

LASCIVIOUS WORDS FROM THE MERCK MANUAL

THE *MERCK MANUAL* IS THE BIBLE OF the medical profession. If a doctor is puzzled by your symptoms, he either prays, calls on a colleague, or looks in the *Manual*. It contains over 2500 pages, listing most of the afflictions that the human body can be heir to — arranged by symptoms, diagnosis, and treatment.

It is rich with the obscure language of the profession ("hypophosphatemia," "ADRs," "ileitis," "hemorrhagic telangiectasia.") Unless you're a professional, you can try to read the volume, but you'll probably find yourself wading about in linguistic hip-boots, ducking an occasional morbidity here and a morphology there.

The medical profession, like the legal, or engineering, or bookkeeping, hides behind obscure and esoteric language. However (and this is what gives one pleasure in going through it,) there is more to the *Merck Manual* than big words and disgusting symptoms. There's poetry in the language, words like "squamous," "thrombosis," "pulpitis." Too, there is a feel for the history of medicine — with such phrases as "pigeon breeder's lung," "Goodpasture's syndrome," "habit spasms," "proud flesh," or one of my favorites — "cri du chat syndrome" (translated as "cat's cry" — one of the early symptoms of mental retardation).

Then there's the mystery of such phrases as "geographic tongue," "port-wine stain," "fiery serpent," or the "fifth disease." (The first is a benign inflammation; the second a type of birthmark; the third a horrible worm that has to be drawn from the skin with a fragile leash over a period of days; the fourth — or is it the fifth? — is but a slight rash.)

Some of us read through the *Manual* because it is not too different from a fine novel, with a huge cast of characters living in tragedy, sickness, and defeat which can just as easily veer into redemption, cure, and health. Also we've noticed that as we are examining the symptoms of some obscure disease — be it plague, parasite, or inflammation — we find that we begin to develop the very symptoms we are studying. Thus it is not rare for me to be laid low with Krabbe's disease, "lazy leukocyte" syndrome, or a powerful recurrence of that chronic and often very painful housemaid's knee — just because I chanced across them in the *Manual*.

⧗

What started me out on all this was a section of the *Manual* dealing with sexuality. The chapters contain the usual sexually trasmitted diseases, sexual problems, sexual malfunctions, and psycho-sexual ailments. There is, too, the usual infelicitous language to limn one of the greatest experiences of being human, what they call "the generalized muscular tension or contractions such as involuntary pelvic thrusting...followed by *resolution*, a sense of general relaxation, well-being, and muscular relaxation." That's an orgasm in med-talk.

What struck me forcefully in this particular part of the *Manual* was one short passage that says too much about you, me, and men and women of the world we live in: "Since normal biologic response is to ejaculate within 2 min after vaginal penetration and since few women are able to reach orgasm within 2 min, most men must learn how to retard emission and ejaculation." Wow. Thirty-five words to tell us about the single most destructive element in the relation between the sexes. You and I would phrase it slightly differently: "He comes right away, while she needs more time. That's why she's never satisfied. And he doesn't know."

He doesn't know, and she can't — or won't — tell him, because most of us men (disabled, old, "normal," young) don't have monkey's sense about how to make love to women.

⧗

Spinal Network magazine recently ran a fascinating series on sexuality.[4] One of the most interesting articles ("Injection Erections: Risking Health for a Hard-On?") included an interview with Marilyn Lemon, sex therapist at a rehabilitation hospital on the west coast. She reported that many of the uses of papaverine (the injections that stimulate erections in the spinal cord injured) were done not so much for the wife or a lady-friend, but rather to assuage the ego of the male. With one couple, Lemon elicited the following discussion,

> *I recently saw a para and his wife. I asked him, "Who are you getting it up for, you or your wife?" His wife said that wasn't what she wanted. The man was surprised. Females want intimacy, to share feelings, to discuss real issues.*

---

[4]Winter, 1991.

There are whole lives (and whole tragedies) hidden in these few lines: men who want to "get it up and get it off;" women who want tenderness, closeness, feelings — and aren't getting it. A tale rendered all the more poignant by the fact that these two, living together as man and wife, had to come to a stranger to find out their sad secret. As Lemon says,

The woman needs to give. When she can't, she ends up feeling hurt, rejected, and frustrated.

In these columns, I have repeatedly emphasized that love, true love, has to include feeling, gentleness, closeness — and at the heart of it all, tenderness. Males, disabled or no, who ignore these necessities lose not only their love and their lovers, but — ultimately — themselves as well.

GOING MAD

REMEMBER: YOU ARE A MACHINE THAT is not only thinking, and thinking about you (among others) — but is, at the same time — thinking about thinking.

It's a feedback system, and it can, like all feedback mechanisms, lose its governors (and its marbles). It starts innocently enough: you find yourself thinking about some misery — thinking about being Crip, say — thinking about it, and thinking some more, and then some more: and suddenly your thoughts and you spin out of control.

It's called going nuts. We Crips are very prone to this, and it hurts.

There are difficulties in going nuts, and even more in knowing you're going nuts. There are also inordinate difficulties in doing something about it. You are a thinking machine, and you need (as all such machines do) the oil of clarity. But when you start down the spiral, it creates its own forward motion. Like mirrors in a barber shop that stare into each other, the reflections go off into infinity, getting distorted, twisted — turning unrecognizable.

At times like this, you cannot be too sure if you are just being yourself or if you are really going bonkers. Your best friends may not want to tell you (and you certainly can't tell yourself). All the servo-mechanisms are out to lunch, the fail-safe mechanisms you use to protect yourself so long have disappeared into the fog. Words begin to repeat themselves; sentences become inchoate. Thoughts won't stop, won't leave you alone — no matter how you try. There is no there there.

So you merely say, "Perhaps I am a little off," thinking about the unexplained extra hours watching TV, or the mornings that you want to hide under the bedcovers. "Maybe I should do something," you tell yourself, remembering the weird thoughts you been having, repeatedly — the ones that you can tell no one, the ones about dying, or mayhem, or vengeance against youself, or against others. "Maybe I'm going over the edge," you say to yourself, remembering how strange your day-to-day world is becoming, those things you said to that lady in the grocery store (telling her you were a candidate for the next space-shuttle!), or what you did at the bar, something you've never done in public before. Worst of all, you think, "I can't control it." What you mean is, "I can't control myself."

And as you spiral downwards, you begin to wonder who is the "I" that you are dealing with. You wonder what is going on with your brain, and you wonder if it will ever stop. You want to hide it, but it's like pregnancy at the sixth month — it begins to reveal itself, and you can't hide it, no matter how desperately you try.

You have to ask someone, but since madness carries a decided paranoia, the phrase "Even your best friends might not tell you" stirs a special kind of fear in you. We depend on our friends for so many things (advice, loans, companionship, love), but as you begin to visit Edge City, your soul-mates might begin to hide from you, might not tell you what is apparent to everyone but you. And the more you think they are doing that, the more they seem to do it.

"They see I am acting funny or talking strangely," you think, "but why won't they tell me?" Perhaps, you think, they're afraid that if they speak the truth, they'll push you a little further over the edge. Perhaps if you get the courage to ask one of them what's going on, they'll tell your other friends, and that will just further your isolation. "Did you hear what he asked me the other day?" they'll say, shaking their heads. You grow indecisive, unable to put your finger on what this fear is, even though it has begun to run you. Fear becomes part of the problem, and madness forms its own blocks to Doing Something About It. You pretend it isn't there, pretend that you aren't worried, but it won't give you escape, not even the escape of sleep. You feel your wits slipping from you, and the harder you grab at them, the more slippery it all becomes. You hear the black machine whirring at the back of the closet, sending out dark waves that threaten to suffocate you. "I've got to get it out of here," you think (you're scared to go in the closet even to check whether it's there or not; you find yourself wearing three-day-old shirts and last week's pants).

"Maybe I should take a trip," you think. But where would you go? You know that if you went to Butte or Atlantic City or Anaheim or Australia, it would still be there, whirring away behind you. You're scared, too scared to do anything, too scared *not* to do anything. It becomes easier to lie there, your back to the closet, turn up the television, turn it up loud, move as little as possible, stay under the covers, say nothing to anyone, don't answer the telephone, or the door.

You're not alone, of course. You have new friends now — friends like Anguish (suppose I lose control of myself?), Isolation (no one will find me if I lose it completely), Circularity (I can't stop it going round and round, can I?), Depression (I'm so depressed, I'm depressed about being depressed), Self-pity (why is my mind picking on me? Why doesn't it leave me alone? Who is this *I* who is picking on me, anyway?). And, finally, a growing Desperation (I can't take this shit any more — I'm going to kill myself).

Kill the situation. It's too much. I can't take it anymore.

⧗

When you reach this stage, you're more than half-way there.

Because if you are at the place where you can ask yourself if you are going bananas, there is an exit. You are at the place where you can go for help, if you can just create the needed force to save yourself.

It can be the end — or it can be the beginning of freedom. If you can make up no more excuses to keep on hiding, then you have reached the end of one line — and the beginning of a new one.

For once you acknowledge that you are cornered, the walls can begin to fall. What you have to do is pick up the telephone and call someone: The local Independent Living Center, or County Mental Health, or a shrink that you know vaguely from a meeting you once went to, or a friend who admitted going to a psychiatrist. Someone in the family, a friend, one that you trust most of all. The call — the first call. The hardest of them all.

"Aren't I admitting I'm sick?" you wonder. "What will they say?" you think. "They'll think I'm a weakling," you say. "What a relief," you say.

You make the call because you know, at this point, that you don't much care, and because all the other choices are simply dead-ends.

SUICIDE

"I've heard a great deal of nonsense about suicide," my father used to say, "but for a man who kills himself resolutely I've never come across any other feeling but respect. Whether suicide is an act of bravery or not is a question that can only concern those who haven't killed themselves."

— *ANTI-MEMOIRS*
ANDRÉ MALRAUX

W E CLAIM TO HAVE SOME KNOWL-edge of suicide, despite the fact that among all the pursuits of humanity, it is the only one in which the successful practicioners are not around to be interviewed.

We know, for one thing, that people who talk about it often go ahead and do it. We know also that they do it at a time when they seem to be "getting better." Depressions disappear, and morbid and chronically sad people begin to blossom. This is so because they have finally made the decision to put an end to it: they know that their ghastly plight will now be done with. All they have to do is figure out how and when to do it. A cloud has been lifted.

We also know that the majority of suicides are botched, and the results, successful or not, are grisly and heartbreaking.

I have always believed that the best way to do one's self in would be as Jack London's heroes died: falling to sleep in a snowbank in the Far North. When they diagnose me with the final illness — the one that is more trouble that it's worth — I'll buy at ticket to Anchorage on Northwest Orient, and once there, rent a fancy and expensive sports car with hand-controls. I'll wait until dark, then drive out to the nearest glacier.

When I get there, I'll take off my shoes and socks and shirt and pants and (and underwear — never let them catch you dead in dirty or tattered underwear) and all my orthopaedic equipment (for the last time, thank god!) and retire to the nearest snowbank. I will be doing my breathing exercises, and reciting my favorite mantra, "Om mani padme hum."

Jack London always said that the feeling of cold goes away quickly, and the feeling that replaces it is one of sleepy warmth within. It turns into a most gentle passing.

⧗

Depression. Has anyone ever written about what it means, its effect on the soul? Or are depressives just too depressed to write about it?

Depression creates its own shroud that is unwilling to disappear. We take it and we take it and finally we decide that we can't take it any more. And that decision may be our salvation.

Rollo May once said that "The idea of suicide has saved many a life." As long as we know that suicide is there — the final relief valve — we may decide just to keep on. For a while. To see what's around the next corner, over the next hill. To see if there is a way out before there's no-way-out.

There are logical reasons that many of us haven't gone ahead and pulled the trigger when everything turns so bleak. One is quite practical. A small amount of reading on the subject of suicide reveals that one should never use a gun or poison or fall out the window of a building because the chances of blowing it are just *too great*.

Several years ago, *CoEvolution Quarterly*[5] published an extended discussion of suicide as an alternative to life. One of the startling conclusions was that of the many people who attempt suicide, too many fail. This would not be so distressing if they merely failed — but most botched it quite badly: permanent paralysis, face half-blown off, blindness, deafness, broken bones, broken spine, loss of stomach from fumaric poisons, extensive liver and kidney damage. "The body's resiliency is astounding," they concluded.

Thus, to try to kill yourself and fail gets to be a double tragedy. Not only are you still in it (life, that is) you are in it with a body that works worse than the one you tried to get rid of.

The Buddhists, the Hindus, and other religions hold that all life is sacred, whether the life of animals, humans, or the self. As living entities, we are sacred. Anyone who deprives us of life is sinning, and will be punished. The penalty: we must return and live through our lives

<hr>

[5] "How Not to Commit Suicide," by Art Kleiner. *CoEvolution Quarterly*, Summer 1981. Available from Whole Earth, Box 428, Sausalito CA 94966.

again and again. In some Indian religions, the penalty is devastating: they say we must return as the one we have destroyed.

Thus if you kill a person, you have to return to earth as that person (and be destroyed by you). If you kill more than one person, you have to return again and again, as each and every one of them.

This twists the theory of karma to a fare-thee-well. It means that Adolf Hitler, Adolf Eichmann and the entire SS have to come back as the Jews they murdered, the 6,000,000 who were killed between 1933 and 1945 — plus whatever gypsies, homosexuals, and other "undesirables" they destroyed along the way.

They not only get to return as their victims: they get to suffer the pain and misfortune that came to these victims during their sad time on earth. Six million times over. This is called learning compassion the hard way.

This concept of karma includes suicide as well. If you kill yourself, you have to come back as you again — drag through the whole long miserable painful process all over again, again and again, until, finally, you decide not to do yourself in again.

Thus, Sylvia Plath has to return to earth as Sylvia Plath, and Ernest Hemingway as Ernest Hemingway. The same goes for Socrates, Virginia Woolf, Philip K. Dick, Maj. Edw. W. Armstrong (and my old roommate from college, Nick Hoppin, who hung himself in a military barracks in England, in 1960).

I should think that if for no other reason, given the chance, no matter how tiny (we must come back as ourselves again!) that alone should be enough to persuade us that suicide is not the answer for our problems.

✕

Still, and however, you and I know that there are times when it gets to be just too much. The body hurts; your kidneys are going dysfunctional again, and the spasms are worse than ever. It's too much for you — or worse, someone else — to be dragging the body from here to there, and back again. No matter what we do, no matter what we take, the pain is always there, a beast that gives no peace, no hope, no courage, no victory, no way.

Who am I (or anyone, for that matter) to tell you to hang in there when your personal care attendant has not shown up for the third time in a week, when you dread calling somebody in your family (they always sigh and make you feel shitty for even asking for some minor help), when the telephone company is threatening to cut off your telephone because you owe so much, and your social worker — who you figure hates you anyway (as you hate her) — is tied up all week "in the field." Your room stinks worse than it ever has, and the couple next door have been screaming at each other all night, and the kids down the way who used to come see you every day (they don't come around any more) leave their broken toys outside your window so you can remember how much fun it used to be with them.

Pain and fatigue sap what's left of your body, depression sweeps down again and brings such an aching woe that time ceases moving. Drinking is stupid, the drugs they offer you turn you into a beast — and you can't pay for them anyway on your tiny allowance. Regret keeps gnawing at you (why didn't I stop when there was time?) again and again and again — and you've found out the hard way that they have built a social service system not meant to help or rehabilitate — but rather to brutalize, defeat, mock, humiliate, degrade, and, finally (is this what they really want?) to kill. They never promised us a rosegarden, but they never promised us a shitheap either.

You feel so bleak in your soul that your friends don't seem to come around so often. Each day seems to bring a new ache (is everyone blind to the dead-end of sitting and hurting and not being able to escape?) Your body is becoming dysfunctional much faster than you ever thought it would and the things that used to give joy are for nothing now: food tastes like straw, the normal pleasures you once enjoyed are vacant and stupid. You've tried shrinks, the MSWs, PhDs, the psychology grad students they've thrown at you. They know about "dysfunctional behavior patterns" and "bipolar manic disorders" but they don't seem to know shit about a body that will never work again, stuck in a room that has no sunshine, from which there is no escape, a place with mucous green walls and vomit brown carpet, and time weighing so heavy, so very very heavy on your heart.

Your brain goes round and round and it gives you nothing but hate: hate for your body, hate for your life, hate for the world. And forever haunting you are the memories of the lost times of Back Then, when the days and your loves were so golden and the passion so sweet — memories that haunt you with a regret so powerful that it threatens to gut your soul, leaving you a hollow swatch of memories, and nothing more.

You are now ready to die.

Far be it from me to tell you not to investigate, at the very least, the options for dying. After all, what could be less dignified than the years you have faced, will continue to face in such joylessness, all the hope squeezed out of the tube — the tube itself twisted and empty? There are methods of getting out and doing it well.

The Hemlock Society is dedicated to helping people leave this world "with dignity," and there's a branch in most major cities. You only have to look in the telephone book — or call information in the nearest large city — and ask for one of their brochures.

There is no cost or obligation.

And no-one will trace your call.[6]

---

[6]The national office is located at Box 11830, Eugene OR 97440.

GETTING MAD

I GOT POLIO FORTY YEARS AGO. IT WAS AN exasperating experience. It robbed me of my childhood, changed — forever — my relationships with my family, my friends, my body, my psyche, and it gave me a whole new world to contend with: hospitals, doctors, physical and occupational therapists, and, ultimately, psychiatrists.

They say there are five stages that the dying must contend with. I suspect for us Crips, there may be a few more, like Regret, and Total Exhaustion, and Too Damn Much Pain, and Fake Acceptance.[7]

I figure I've gone through them all. Like all of us, I've had to grieve over the death of my body, time and time again — each time, making way for a new body, one completely different.

From my experience over the years, I have learned, too, that these feelings are not independent beasts that come in the night, stay around awhile and then disappear. Rather, they are on-going, ever-present tensions that become a part of our lives. Right now I am angry (I just got back from the store; someone had parked a Cadillac convertible so close to my car that I could scarcely get in the door; I got some sour vengeance, though: I scratched their nice white paint-job with my car-door; but I still was exasperated). And last night, there was regret: at a party, all the kids were dancing like crazy and brawling and jumping about. I found myself, again, regretting (again) the course of my life, the one that had not granted me their grace and ease — to move legs and arms and torsos about without worry, without thinking, without that

---

[7]See Introduction.

infernal plotting and planning, how to move from here to there without causing a scene, stirring up all that attention. "I'm sorry, I'm sorry, I'm sorry," I told myself, regretting a bit the journey I had been on; and not being able to share their stupendous sense of freedom, their easy hilarity.[8]

⧗

Of course, there is, too, righteous and hard-won acceptance. There are times when I accept my body, and its fate, and the world I have created with it. But "acceptance" is tricky: it's like soap in the bathtub. Sometimes you have it; sometimes you think you have it; and sometimes, at times of stress, it just disappears and is nowhere to be found, no matter how hard you search through the murk.

I have long contended that the most profound and oppressive of the banana-bunch of feelings is anger. I will say without any fear of contradiction that it is something we Crips all have. I'll go further and say that anger is something many of us become experts at hiding. In fact, some of us hide it so well that we don't even know it is there inside us.

Anger is a form of murder, and like murder, it stays hidden until we ourselves reveal it. As Inspector Poirot says, "A human being...cannot resist the opportunity to reveal himself and express his personality which conversation gives him. Every time he will give himself away."

When I say "anger," I am not talking about those towering rages that erupt so devastatingly in some of us. Rather, I am talking about the fire underground — that

---

[8]In one of the poignant passages in *The Body Silent,* Murphy, now in his new wheel-chair, watches an athlete, bursting with youth and vitality, running by his living-room window. "There but for the grace of God go I," he says.

conflagration that eats away at the coal fields for decades, only occasionally volleying forth with smoke, the rest of the time hidden, destroying the vitals. The people in the village deny its very existence until one of the houses bursts into flame and smoke.

After forty years of watching myself and my peers, I will offer you a point of fact: we are all angry. Worse, I know only a few who will confess to this anger. Most say, "Who me? Angry? What *are* you are talking about?" Gregory Bateson said that denial was bad enough, but denial of denial is the real soul-destroyer.

⧗

So what does this mean to you? If you have anger (as I claim you do) what should you do about it? And where did it come from, anyway?

Let's answer the last question first. Our whole American society is geared towards health, well-being, the Pepsi Generation, beauty, youth, mountain climbing, jogging, perfection of body and soul. It is hard for us to be free from the oppressive feeling that something is wrong with us because we who don't have perfect bodies, we don't have the ability to go anywhere and do anything we want. They have it, we don't (and they probably don't give a toot about us, either). Further, despite what the activists say, there is and always will be a part of us that regrets — for some bitterly, for some more gently — our differences from the rest of the world.[9]

---

[9]It is also possible that our anger — the deepest, the most unreachable anger — is in place because we know too much. We Crips have been branded (in the most tender part of our souls) with a knowledge of the powerful vulnerability of body, and the extreme fragility of health. Since fear = anger, our very wisdom terrorizes us into *rage*.

How can you know that this rage is there? I offer some very simple tests. You can try them on yourself, by asking the people closest to you (find those who won't lie to you when you ask them a direct question) and by keeping a diary for a few months, honestly noting down the following:

1) Do friends or lovers come and go — to the point of not being there when you need them?

2) Do you get drunk or stoned often? (You yourself have to define "often;" you even have to define "drunk or stoned;" low alcohol drinks like beer or wine, or regularly prescribed drugs can be a device for hiding yourself from yourself).

3) Do you show a bitterness in your words — a cynicism, a sarcasm, a down-home nastiness that helps to distance others from you: in other words, are you the life of the party until the party disappears? Noting down exact conversations and reviewing them weeks later can be very revealing.

4) Do you get depressed often? (Depression is that dark feeling that makes it impossible to function — the cloud or curtain over experiences, experiences that should be joyful.)

5) How do you react when someone says, "You seem a little pissed off?" (If you get angry at being accused of being angry — that's a dead giveaway).

6) Do you ever think of suicide to the point of plotting out the exact method of doing it, even writing out the note you will leave behind?

7) Do you have any of what they call non-specific illnesses not related to being Crip (and you have to search carefully, for you and I can blame almost everything on our physical condition): headaches, backaches, stomach-aches,

vague nausea, inability to sleep — and the real test, recurring nightmares?

8) Are you always, always, always cheerful? (They say "How does he do it? He's so wonderful.") I'm not here to be Dr. Doom, but the eternally cheerful Crips either have achieved sainthood — or are lying. If you are in the first category, you shouldn't be wasting your time reading this book. If you are in the second — you should begin serious work on escaping from behind the mask.

⧗

What can we do for ourselves to diminish this anger?

I have always recommended counseling (if you get angry when someone suggests you should see a shrink, that's another giveaway).

Individual counseling with psychiatrists, psychologists, and social workers is great — but it may cost more than you can afford. You might look to group therapy, which is the cheapest and can be the best. It means that you will be talking about common problems with your peers — people who live and feel and work daily with the same problems you do.[10]

The reason that shrinks and counseling are still around after a hundred years is because, for many people, they work. And — for those of us with expert and intricate systems of denial — they may be the only way out. (Suicide, madness and continual depression are other ways out, but I

---

[10]Every Independent Living Center (Centers for the Disabled) offers peer group counselling. There is a central clearing house — with names, addresses, and telephone numbers. For $8.50 they will send you their latest volume with over 400 names and addresses. Ask for the Independent Living Research Utilization Directory. Write to: ILRU, Room 1000, 2323 S. Shepherd, Houston TX 77019

do not suggest them as viable alternatives. They hurt too much.)

Don't worry about whom to see. Take it on faith that will take care of itself. The horror stories about counselings that have gone awry, counselors who are abusers (or, at best, simply incompetent) — all these have an element of truth. But I assure you that these are not the majority. Successful "interventions" (that's what they are called) are the rule rather than the exception.

For those of us with this unbearable itch called anger, (the itch that can be as unbearable as the itch of lust) counseling may be the only way out. Listen to yourself at this very instant. What's going on in your head as you are reading this? If you are saying "That's not for me," or "I'm not gonna waste three hours (and $80) a week on talking to some geek," or "I can't afford it!" — then you are denying yourself a great chance for freedom. Or, at the least, a retreat from the horror show that emotional pain can bring. By going before the mirror and truly, for the first time, seeing yourself — seeing that scared child lying within — you can open youself to a whole other life. If you so choose.

⧗

"This is stupid — just stupid," I yelled at one of my shrinks not long ago. "What the hell am I doing here paying you $80 an hour just to blab? I must be nuts."

He says nothing.

"Do you really think we can go at it like this and get me any better?"

"Did you say 'go at it?...'"

"Yeah, that's it — it's a battle, a fight. With you, it's always a battle."

"I suspect that you're not fighting me," he says. "Maybe you're fighting you. I'm just the referee."

"Referee, my ass," I say, "You're more like a goad. Or a toad. And you don't seem to have gotten rid of these goddamn depressions. I'm still hurting. And you don't care, do you?" Pause. "Are you some kinda quack?"

"Probably," he says. I have an urge to hit him when he says that, but it's hard to throw a real haymaker from a wheelchair. Besides, I'm a member of the Nonviolent Movement of the Brothers of Non-Movement, so I content myself with glaring at him.

"Then what the hell am I doing here?"

"That's a good question," he says. "I'm probably not here to get rid of your depressions. You have to get rid of them yourself. And what we can best hope for is not to eliminate them — that would be impossible — but to take the edge off them, so that they aren't so life-threatening, so you don't have to go around telling me you're going to kill yourself everytime you have some bitch of a problem."

There's a pause. He smiles a bit.

"Sometimes I think you're the nut case," I say. "You really are a quack. Have you ever thought of going to a shrink?"

"How do you think I ever got here?" he says. "Besides, I have to be a quack to put up with you, don't you think?"

Silence.

"Sometimes I think you should put me away so I can get some peace," I say, still sulking.

"Put you away? Institutionalize you?" He rolls his eyes. "Good Lord, man — are you *crazy!*"
We both giggle.

II. ARTICLES

" *We Crips have an astonishing freedom that we scarcely ever acknowledge. It's that most of the world will not mess with us.*

" *The able-bodied can be torn apart by crowds (or the police), robbed, beaten, abused in public or in their homes. For the most part, we are exempt from this. Our wheelchairs, walkers, skewed hands, bent legs — our very way of moving — are barriers to others' violence.*

" *Our dysfunctional bodies give us extraordinary freedom to go where we please and do what we want. We may scorn the pity that is projected onto us, but in most parts of the world, it serves to protect us from even the most hardened heart.*"

— *AUTHOR'S NOTEBOOK, 1984*

LORENZO W. MILAM

EATING HEAD

We are in a cosmic realm, a realm older than religion.
The idea of the creation of the world has probably not
yet been conceived. They kill in the eternal. The gods
have not yet been born...

ANTI-MEMOIRS

JESÚS'S FAVORITE ICE-CREAM IS PIS-
tachio, but sometimes he likes the *nuez,* vanilla swirls
with little bits of nut. He orders it for us, and then we
sit and eat it and watch the people go by on the street of
Puerto Perdido. Jesús worked for me last year when I was
here, my first winter in Oaxaca. He and his friend Diego
are taking care of me this year. Jesús works Monday
through Friday; Diego works on his days off.

Jesús and I are watching the pale Americans, the
drunken Americans, the loud Americans, the unlovely
Americans. Intermixed with them are the betel nut Mix-
tecs and Zapotecs — boys with buckets full of fish, women
carrying brown-eyed babies, children running and laughing, old men dressed, still, in traditional white shirts and
huaraches.

"Gringo watching," I call it, but I'm also watching
the Mexicans, because of my prejudice. I've been living in
Mexico on and off for twenty years, and slowly I'm devel-
oping this prejudice, this terrible prejudice, against pale
skin. "American's are so pale and wan — in such a hurry," I
think, trying to forget that I'm one of them. Jesús isn't
prejudiced. He watches the young ladies, watches them all.
Those from north of the border are as interesting to him as

those from his own home town. He wants them all. He has just turned eighteen.

This morning we had our first rain in almost six months. This is a drought area, and the hills have turned sere. I often wonder that the whole area doesn't come down with some great fever from the sky: a grand conflagration that will burn up the fields, take the city of Puerto Perdido and the tourists, take them up in one smoky mass. Anyway, the rain changes all that, turns the fields dark, fills the air with the smell of whetted ashes.

"What's it like being here, in Mexico, in a wheel-chair?" The lady asking this question is thirty, thirty-five years old. Her chin is sharp and pointed, her face pale, eyes hidden behind large dark glasses. I am watching the balloon-man across the plaza. He has balloons in all sizes and shapes, floating in a bunch above his head, on strings. I favor the "monstro," the monster head, a funny face with squiggly balloons sprouting over the top of it. I wonder how he makes it look so — well — *human.*

"I have a brother in a wheelchair," she says. "He's a quad. That's why I'm asking." Throaty voice, no accent. She must be from the west. A brother who's a quad. "I've got a brother who's a quad." They always say that. Or: "My mother has diabetes, they took off her leg right here," (slicing motion across the thigh). We hear that a lot. "My uncle's in a wheelchair. Viet Nam." The non-specific description. Or the very specific: "My dad is a stroke victim and his whole side is useless — he uses a cane and we have to feed him." All these cripples. A world full of cripples. And we get to hear about all of them. As if we wanted to know; as if we really cared.

I always wonder why absolute strangers come up to me to tell me these stories about people I don't know, will never know, can never care about. "I have enough troubles without this," I think. "They are just trying to reach out, the only way they know how," I tell myself. "You're not alone," they are saying, certain that I feel alone. "I know someone who's just as bad off as you," they're saying. "Don't you feel better now?" they think.

Maybe I am softening. I don't pretend I'm a deaf-mute any more, when they start in on their relatives. I don't — as I did, the last time I was here — pretend that I speak no English. *"Lo siento — no entiendo los gabachos,"* I said. ("Sorry, I don't understand Americans.") There were times, I admit, when I just looked at them, and said "Oh?" or, nodding my head, "Mmm." Then I let it die.

Thirty-five years have probably softened me, made me more willing to listen: People hurting, everywhere people hurting. This lady hurting, with whatever it is that our families feel: angst, maybe; fear, possibly; guilt, certainly. "Anytime anyone talks to you, it is God talking to you, telling you something you need to hear right now," Stephen Gaskin used to say — but sometimes I wonder if the words are garbled, the messenger a little befuddled. What to respond? I know, in 1952 or 1966 or 1974, you couldn't get a whisper out of me on this "my brother's a quad" business. Now, it's different. *The idea of the creation of the world has probably not yet been conceived...*

"It's the same," I say. "No: that's not exactly right. It's complicated and it can be frustrating. But there are things to compensate for it," I tell her. (Is this really me?) "Like my two employess. Jesús's been working for me for a couple of winters now, Diego started a few weeks ago."

They take me about Puerto Perdido, to the river, or to the beach, to swim. They get me out of the car and down to the water — and then back out again, rinsed off, into the car, home again.

"They buy my food for me at the public market (inaccessible), help me cook it (I'm learning to cook black beans and rice), even help me eat it," I tell her. "They help me a great deal," I tell her. Two employees. What does that mean? Two young people who are becoming part of my life here, so far from home. Diego with his dark polished skin, his careful walk, his straight Mayan nose, his serene face. Jesús with the rounded god's head, right out of the Yucatan, the great slow eyes, the eyes he rolls about so when I ask him to do something he doesn't especially want to do.

"They're fun to be with," I tell her. They are filled with that strange mixture of Mexican manhood and sentiment that fascinates me. "They might be the best part of my stay here," I say. "They're very good workers. They're with me every day. Nights, too. I pay them $35. That's more than the minimum wage here." Jesús, who makes me laugh when I am feeling blue. "¿Qué pasa, gabacho?" What's going on, he asks me, at those times when I don't feel like going out. "¡Qué pasa — tú!" You — what's happening? And if I don't say anything, they work on me some more, and the two of them manage, somehow, to get me up, and out the door. I don't protest, not too much. Once I get to the ocean's edge, I can't be thinking those thoughts any more, can I?

"They teach me Spanish," I tell her. "I'd have to pay Berlitz a fortune for the lessons they give me for free." Then I tell her about the frustrations. Mexico isn't set up for wheelchairs. Not many ramps, almost no curb-cuts. There are very few hotels that have rooms for the disabled. I had to scout out the five restaurants (of twenty) in Puerto Perdido that we can get to without having to go up or down steep stairs. I have yet to get over my unwillingness to be carried in and out of restaurants, bathrooms, banks.

"It's a concession to being in a Third World Country," I tell her. "With my helpers, it doesn't have to be a big deal." They like showing off their strength, and they can be very funny about it. "Pinche Gringo," Jesús will say. "Pesa 400 kilos." That means he thinks I weigh 850 pounds. When he says that, I think it is his way of telling me he likes me: when he calls me "Pinche Gringo."

"There's no special parking, or special placards," I tell her. "But when I park my car on the beach, so I'm near the water, the police never bother me." I think of how they would do it in California, or Florida, or Texas. It's against the law, just as it is here, so the police there would probably give me a $250 ticket, and apologize for doing it.

"Sometimes, I feel like a mountain climber here," I say. Quite suddenly the sky turns iridescent, then a brilliant magenta. The usual spectacular tropical sunset that happens so quickly. Even when you're expecting it, it's a surprise — the sudden end of the searing heat and too-bright sunlight. "How'd he get to be a quad?" I ask her. The street turns dim and dusty. I can no longer see her face, only the outline of her head, the tiny round gold medal around her neck. She is still wearing her dark glasses. She tells me about the drinking, and the general helling around when he was twenty. The drugs, the accident. "They didn't know whether he was going to live," she says. "He made it." She pauses. "I think he's a much better person for it," she says.

I look at the balloon man. He's standing under the one streetlight of Puerto Perdido. The light has just come on, so the balloons cast a dark cloud over him. There are many of them straining up on their strings — and he is such a tiny fellow that I half expect to see him take off, floating away into the starry sky, rising up into the stratosphere. Our balloonman which art in heaven.

"A much better person," I say, nodding. "That's an awful thing to say."

"I'm sorry?" She's not apologizing — she just doesn't understand.

"I can't stand hearing that sort of thing," I say. She turns her head to watch the balloon man. He creates his monsters right there, out of rubber and helium. He fills the balloons from the great bruised silver tank at his side, twists them into animal faces, or strange bodies, twisting and turning this way and that. When he fills the balloons with the helium, it makes a raw, screeching sound. She sits down on the curb next to me.

"I don't understand," she says, "...but maybe I never will. I don't know. I just don't have your experience." She tells me that she is a professional nurse, living in Colorado. She says that even with her training, the hardest job was learning to deal with her brother's body. "I'm a nurse by training. I've done caths — lots of times. And yet, nothing is harder for me," she says. She stops. "He was the one that used to pick on me all the time, never had any time for me, called me 'stupid.' And now there he is, lying flat on his bed. Sometimes I have to give him his catheter in the morning. And he can't even cover himself up..."

A little girl, she can't be more than five years old, is trying to push two boys, probably her brothers, up the hill, in a tiny scratched red wooden wagon, with warped wheels. One of the boys, the older one, is yelling "*¡Recio, recio!*" (faster, faster!) The other one is just sitting there, at the front of the wagon, without a stitch on, just digging the hell out of his ride. The girl can barely get it to move, what with the hill and all: she's pushing with all her might.

"I don't even know what I mean," I say. "About those words — 'maybe he's better for it.' I don't think it's up to us to say that sort of thing." What is it they say? *Only the gods can worship god.* Only the gods can pass judgment on those who are different…so different from the rest of humanity.

Jesús is behind me now. He is pushing back and forth on the wheelchair, slowly, rhythmically. There's a fiesta in Pinotepla. He wants to get over there, to check on a young lady who he claims will be his next "novia." He wants to get me over there because he knows that by ten, when things are starting to happen, I'll be drunk, and insist on going home to bed. He doesn't want to miss a thing. I went to the Pinotepla Fiesta before, once last year. The ground is sandy, people will be pushing in on my wheelchair from all sides. We'll get stuck, people will stare. From two feet away they'll stop dead and stare. They always do. I'm probably the only six-foot gringo they've ever seen in a wheelchair in their town — possibly the only one they'll see in this part of Mexico.

Given all the bother, I probably wouldn't even go…if it weren't for the fact that when I'm there, I'm living. Going out in the world, seeing a different world. The lady wants to know if her brother in his wheelchair would be happy here. "Sure," I want to tell her, "it'll be all right if he doesn't mind getting stuck, having people gaga staring at him, kids standing, just staring at him. It's all right, if you don't mind being a freak." I want to tell her that. But that sounds bitter — and it would probably be a lie. There aren't many of us around, and we're the object of curiosity; but it's a curiosity coming from some of the kindest, sweetest, most open, free people in the whole world. I think of my times here, the despair that occasionally comes from the inaccessible buildings, places I can't ever dream of getting up to, or down from: the times that my bladder is bursting, and there's no place to go, and I want to cry out, or just cry. And Jesús, with his great, wise, serious eyes, understanding, somehow, always figuring out what is going on, figuring a way for me to make it, without going balmy.

"It's a whole different world down here," I tell her. "Your brother might like it, or, then again, he might despise it. You can never tell. It depends on him, and how much he likes Mexico, and Mexicans." I think about what happened this morning. I was feeling a bit blue, and so Jesús started in pinching me, and then ducking away when I tried to grab him. He saw I was turning a bit sour, and he wanted to be sure I got my daily quota of tickles and pinches. I wonder if the attendants in the United States — what do they call them? "the personal care attendants" — I wonder if they are allowed to tickle their charges when they start to feel bad. Is pinching written into an attendant's job description? A good thorough tickling when the patient starts to feel bad?

"To me — they're all gods, so I forgive them everything," I say. I think of Jesús, with his great round face, that monumental face out of the tombs of Quintana Roo — the lids so heavy, the lips so broad, so compassionate, the eyes so inexpressively expressive. Jesús with the elegant Mayan nose, his wry, gentle way with me. *The gods have not yet been born.*

"What do you mean by that?" she asks, moving her hands vaguely. I wonder if I can get it across. "To be here, to get into the country, you have to be willing to leave your set behind, leave behind *gringoismo* — the American ice.

"And you can't just do it for a week or a month. You have to do it longer," I say. "There's something special going on here. We might call it 'love' — but I think there might be other...better words.

"Mexicans learn to love so quickly and easily, no matter how unlovable we may be — to them, or to ourselves," I say. "Some of us — if we are lucky — learn to love them in return, without reserve. We gringos are so much slower, so much more fearful. We call it love, but for Americans, it's more like taking hostages. Especially for those of us..." I want to say "for those of us like your brother and me..." but I don't finish the sentence.

Over where the sun has died on the horizon, there is a bare smudge of rouge, a burning off, so far off. "It's god-love," I think. "The gods know it well." I look at her. She's standing up, brushing off her skirt. "It's hard for us to learn about them," I say. "Sometimes we wonder what's left for us..." I start to say, but she has already smiled, turned — and is gone. I'm still talking, still formulating whatever it is I am supposed to be saying, and she's gone. I think of that line from Beckett: *The trouble with her was that she had never really been born."*

⧗

An hour later, Jesús and I are smack-dab in the middle of the Pinotepla Fair. Just as I thought: I get stuck in the sand twice, and at least 300 people give me a good going-over, not just looking, but staring. And, yes, Jesús has talked me into eating several *tacos de cabeza*. Brain tacos. "It's all right if you don't mind eating all those thoughts," I tell my friends later. "It's supposed to make you smarter."

"*¿Quién fue esta mujer?*" Jesús asks me. Who was that woman? He thinks, naturally, that I should make her my *novia*, eventually marry her. He thinks I should marry every woman I meet, settle down. He starts to look for his girlfriend in the crowd. I get a glimpse of her. She has long black hair, tied in a single long thick strand, interwoven with a length of bright red wool. Her eyes are as deep and as mysterious as his own, her skin the color of butter chocolate.

"*No sé*," I say. I don't know. "*Otra gringa*," I say. "*Poquita confusada.*" A little confused. "*Como todo.*" Another American woman. A little confused. Just like the rest of us.

THIS SPACE RESERVED FOR MANIC-DEPRESSIVES ONLY

I HAD READ AN ARTICLE ABOUT HER IN the local paper. They said she specialized in burn-out. That's what I thought I had. It took me a while to figure out the truth, but she probably knew the moment I came in the door.

I drove up to her house on the hill there in the south-eastern part of La Jolla. The front yard consisted of an arty black wrought-iron fence and a black inverted tin-can with holes in the sides stuck on a pole. That was the light fixture. Then there were these heavy slabs of terra-cotta jammed in the wall for an artificial water-fall (which wasn't working). There was dirty, peeling Astro-Turf. The light can was stuck in the middle of the Astro-Turf.

She had poodles. Not the big ones; no — those little white ones with pink asses and ribbons in their hair and yappy barks. "Just like my mother," I thought. My mother, as long as I can remember, has always had poodles. They fight with each other, get underfoot. One of them is seventeen years old, with bad breath and phlebitis. The others are card-carrying hebephrenics.

Those dogs — that was the first thing I ran into when I came into Rachael's office. The second one was me. Rachael kept asking me why I was there, and I told some of these funny stories about me and my burn-out, and while I was talking, this tear came out of her left eye, ran down her cheek. Rachael sat there in front of me, immediately after I had delivered one of my funniest lines, and this tear came down and I thought, "She's crying." Then I wondered, "What have I said wrong?" I was looking for a solution to my burn-out and I ran into this thirty-five-year-old shrink who has freckles and poodles and still knows how to cry.

⧗

Rachael's mother had polio, just like me. A long time ago they burned out part of her body and soul, and for replacement they gave her all these parts: rods, leather, moleskin, wires, straps, chairs with wheels. Like me they gave her all these parts — along with a fictive heart — to keep her alive. Most people notice the metal and wheels and leather, but they miss the heart-job. We get so good at it they don't even notice.

It's not like we were doing this for our health, mind you. You know the trips they put on us when they see our crutches and our wheelchairs, see us go up the stairs, getting around with our hands. When they see that, there are all these rude things they lay on us. Going on about their uncles or dads or brothers and sisters, about their own failing legs or arms, their operations (sometimes they'll stop right there in front of the bank and roll up sleeves, raise up the pantslegs, to show us the scars.) And fifty gets you ten they start in about Jesus, and How Much He Loves Us. The things they do to us, without even an iota of regard, courtesy, respect for *our* privacy...

And in counterpoint (a reflection) there're these things we do to them, not to say to our own families, and to ourselves. Rachael knew, because she had been there before. Her mother, with all these shields and mirrors, so people wouldn't be trying to get too close to her, with their nonsense. You've been there — you know what I am talking about.

After all, somewhere in our lives we've had to learn a new balancing act. We've had to learn to keep people out of our way so we won't get tripped up. And we get good, most of us: with our words, with a gesture, with a look — we keep things in control. To be in control without appearing to be in control — that's what it's all about, right?

At the time of my first meeting with Rachael, I thought these tricks were peculiar to me. They were so well a part of me that even I, their progenitor, could barely see them. I figured she couldn't either. I had spent many years honing them to sharp perfection — the secret craftsman in the dark attic.

Turns out she had seen all this sleight-of-hand before, and the first time we met she was telling me how well I was doing. At the same time, she was telling me how much it hurt. All of us.

After I had been seeing her for two months, I told her my Park Guard story. It was one of my favorite Cripstories. We're at Desert Hot Springs, Frank and Janet and Leslie and I, and it's eight in the morning. We've been up all night watching the stars in the Anza-Borrego State Park, and we drive into the springs area and strip off our clothes and they help me to get over to the pool, the warm waters, where we swim for a while — but someone complains, so this Park Guard comes out with his eyes flashing and he says "No skinny-dipping. Out!"

So the others get out of the pool, and Frank reaches for me but I shoo him away, so I can get out of the pool myself. The guard is standing there, and I drag myself out as slowly as possible: it takes me at least five minutes to pull myself over to my clothes, and then slowly, oh so slowly, I get the clothes on — all while he's watching. "I could've done it in a minute with Frank's help," I tell Rachael, later, "but I wanted that son-of-a-bitching guard to suffer."

"But why did you do it?" she says.

"You'd do the same thing if you were me," I say.

"You've said that before," she says.

"It's true. Don't you see? No, you don't. All I can tell you is that you would do the same thing if you were me."

"I think I understand, but I want to be sure you do," she says. "I'm going to make a sign, and you're going to wear it for the next twenty-four hours."

"Oh stop it, Rachael," I tell her. I've had to put up with a whole passel of her nonsense these last two months, but this certainly took the cake.

She takes a piece of cardboard, and with a black Magic Marker she writes

**YOU'D DO THE SAME THING
IF YOU WERE ME.**

She takes thread, puts two holes in the top of the sign, and threads it so it can hang around my neck. She tells me to wear it for the next twenty-four hours. Wherever I go, I'll have that damn sign hanging on me for people to look at.

To the people I was living with — there in the commune on Third Avenue — it didn't make any difference. Half of them were going through Fisher-Hoffman, or *est*, or some kind of freaky training, so they were used to these nutty things, like the guy upstairs who had to carry teddy bear around with him for a month. It was the people at the It'll Do Tavern that worried me. I went there every night, at eight, for hamburger and beer, to play pinball (it was about all I could do during that Year of the Angst — go to my shrink, eat hamburgers, drink beer, and play pinball).

"What are they going to say when I come in with this dumb sign around my neck?" I fretted. I almost didn't go — but then, there was this other part of me that wanted to see what they would say, how they'd react.

I needn't have worried. They checked out the sign for a full five seconds and then went right back to arguing about the Boston Reds. "What did you guys think was happening?" I asked Bill the barkeep as he was closing up. "We thought you'd joined a fraternity," he said. "We thought it was some kinda joke, maybe some kinda initiation you was in."

He was right. It was an initiation. It just wasn't the one we had imagined.

In the official lingo of the shrink trade, many of us drag around something called "Entitlement." "You don't know — you just don't know — you don't have a *clue*," is what we say to ourselves, to others. They — family, friends, strangers — may try to imagine what's going on inside us, but they'll never know. Even my shrink, even with her mother, even after all this time — I knew she didn't know what was going on inside of me, not really. No one knows what it's like to wake up in the morning with this body: to move the way we move, to feel the way we feel, to have people laying these trips on us. We figure we have something special, something they don't and can't and will never have.

This specialness gives us certain freedoms. Society awards some of them (special parking, special entrances, special support). We arrogate more for ourselves. I can run that number on the Park Guard, or be pissed-off, angry, cruel because everybody else in the world "would do the same thing if they were me."

I now suspect that entitlement underlies much anti-social behavior — alcoholism, familial violence, abuse (physical or mental), martyrdom, stuck families. It certainly is the operating mode for a certain types of rage: knife-slashing sarcasm, emotional violence perpetuated by us on others (and by others on us.) We give it to our families, to our friends, and to strangers. And sometimes they give it back to us — in spades.

I didn't get the message of the sign for a while. It went everywhere with me for a full day and a full night, and I still didn't get it. It did get stored away in my brain-pan, though. Everytime I opened my mouth to say it, the buzzer would go off. I wasn't sure *why* I shouldn't say it — I just knew enough not to any more. It wasn't until I got involved in the gun incident that it began to make sense to me.

For the longest time, one of my favorite tricks was the Big Block. It works like this: I go over to the Post Office, and there's this guy in his late model grey Mercedes parked in the Handicapped Parking Space. He doesn't have a sticker or anything; he's just in a hurry. So what I do is I pull in right behind him, blocking his way out. I wait for him to come out of the Post Office, then, slowly — oh so slowly — I get out of my car. (As with the Park Guard, my operating efficiency drops to about 10% because I want that son-of-a-bitch to suffer.)

I get over to him, while he's waiting there, stewing, and I say: "You know, this is always a problem for me. (Pause.) When you park in that space, I have to park way over there…" (I motion over to the far part of the parking lot.) And then, not even waiting for his answer, slowly, slowly, I work my way back to my car. Your friendly local representative of The Crip Police.

The last time I did it was at the Safeway, a year ago. The guy had a sporty black Corvette. I waited for him to come out of the store. As he was getting into his car, I started into my spiel, but he told me that I had better move my ass out of his way "at once, bro." There was something in his eyes, the way he looked at me: I went back to my car, got out of there faster than usual.

As I was backing up, some long-haired drifters decided to take up the cudgel for me — which is not unlike having the Ku Klux Klan come out in favor of one of your pet social programs. As the Corvette was backing up, they ran over and called the driver several unsavory names, started kicking at the door of his car. The driver sped out of there, and in three minutes was back with a big .45. The long-hairs got out of there much faster than I thought they would. And me? When the policeman finally came, I was inside, pretending to examine the Marie Callander pies. My voice was still shaking as I told him my side of the story. I didn't tell him everything, though. Like the fact that I had blocked the Corvette's exit. Or that I would never do it again.

⧗

I was raised and educated a Quaker. Recently, I have been drawn back to it, and — at the same time — developed an interest in some of the more remote Eastern religions.

One of the basic tenets of these religions is that the divine lies within all of us (inside me, inside you, inside Rachael, the park guard, the owner of the Corvette, the two drifters, the cop). He's not out there somewhere above, yanking on His beard and stewing about us doing wrong. He (or She — accounts differ) lounges about inside of us, watching, nodding, a part of all our good and bad deeds, not judging, not condemning: just watching.

Another of their tenets is right out of Newton's Third Law. To every action, there's an equal and opposite reaction. If I do something good, something good will flow from it. If I do something selfish, cruel, entrapping — an equally selfish, cruel, entrapping action will flow from it, and will ultimately come back to me.

Thus I may think I am entitled to do certain things, like blackmailing people with my body. But I am a fool to think there will be no kickback. Entitlement is spawned by anger, not by justice, and it will spawn anger. If we use it, it rises up, somehow, to reward us. The reward is not always so good.

This doesn't stop me from feeling pissed-off when they pull the old strings. Last week, I drove into the Safeway parking lot, and there it was, a ratty old Valiant parked in "my" place — no disabled plates, nothing.

As I was getting out of my car, a guy in a sporty houndstooth jacket dashed out of the store, got in the Valiant.

"Hey," I yell at him. "That's a disabled parking spot. Can't you read the sign?"

"Don't get on my case, buddy." His face wasn't any too friendly.

"Yeah, but I need that space."

"You're not the only one who needs that space, you know, buddy?"

"Oh?" He didn't *look* very disabled.

"Yeah — I deserve it too. I'm a manic-depressive, so don't get on my case, buddy."

With that, he pops in his car and he's gone.

Well, he had me there. Who am I to say that he is better or worse off than the rest of us, has any more or less rights than us, with all our entitlements?

LORENZO W. MILAM

A NOTE ABOUT PILLS FROM YOUR FRIENDLY NEIGHBORHOOD GENTEEL CRIP JUNKY

G IVE ME A PILL AND I AM HAPPY. GIVE me two, and I am ecstatic. Give me three, and you have a friend for life.

Not just any pill, of course. It has to be an analgesic. Codeine. Darvon. Maybe Percodan — although they're awful strong. You can skip the Demerol or Dilantin: I want to laugh and sing and enjoy life — not dump it. If you give me Xanax (now the most favored tranquilizer), I'll probably just store it at the back of the medicine cabinet. I don't like turning into a cow. I may be just your typical neighborhood genteel crip junkie — but I want to be happy, not stupid.

I got all these anti-social attitudes on drugs from growing up in the sixties, and from listening to messages from my body, and from *Consumers Reports*. No kidding.

I don't have to tell you about the sixties. They have movies to tell you what we thought we were doing to the world — and ourselves — in the flowerpower years.

My body? Well, let me say this about that. It's out-to-lunch, has been so since I got polio in 1952. And all these years haven't helped it worth shit. Walking on crutches — like I did full-time for thirty years until I returned to the wheelchair — has induced arthritis in the shoulders and knees, funny shooting pains in the arms and hands. Falling again and again has turned my face and my body into a battle zone. Years of living with braces, wheel-chairs, and back-support corsets leave all sorts of sores behind, and there is never a moment — standing, sitting, or lying down — when I feel comfortable. Man-made mobile, seating, and walking equipment can never be comfortable. After all, it is a substitute, and you remember what substitutes do to us.

Finally, there's *Consumers' Reports*. Several years ago, in one of their books on drugs, they reported several facts about heroin that I had never read anywhere before.[11] One was that it was probably one of the best all around pain-killers available, and they suggested that it was a misguided mistake that we didn't make it available for those in terminal pain. In other words, we let the FDA and a bunch of thoughtless bureaucrats (not to say thoughtless junkies) interdict a very humane method for pain-control. In this respect, we differ sharply from the English, who still permit heroin use for cancer patients.

The other part of the *CU* report described "week-end" heroin users — those who weren't interested in being junkies, but who enjoyed the effect of casually using the drug. These were, it was reported, by far its largest con-sumers. What was surprising was that for this bunch, there was apparently no need to get hooked. They're just people who get a bang out of being stoned on what is, after all, one of the most powerful drugs of all time. Their use is casual, their attitude unrepentant, the results — non-fatal.

---

[11]*U. S. Pharmacopeia Drug Information for the Consumer,* Consumers Union, Mt. Vernon NY; 1987.

For better or worse, I am not very interested in heroin. I figure I am one of those people who would find it *just too good*, and I would probably end up sticking it in my arm for the rest of my life — knocking over 7-11's after midnight and stealing little girls' bicycles so I could feed my habit.

For that reason, I content myself with pills. I like pills better than martinis, Virginia Slims, cheesecake, the Mamas and the Papas, and Doritos. Give me a Darvon or Talwin with codeine — I usually take them with my afternoon beer — and I'm happy as a clam for the rest of the day and much of the night.

Unfortunately, they don't make it easy for us to follow that regimen. They want us to suffer with our aches. When I call my doctor for another prescription for analgesics, the messages tend to get lost. When I finally do get through, you can hear the edge in his voice. He'll write one prescription (a small one), charge $45 for it, and won't honor any further requests unless I can show a broken leg, the Yaws, or imminent death.

In other words — in America (land of the free) it is immoral to avoid pain for a lifetime. We're all John Waynes, right? They want to be sure that I feel bad for ducking out from the required day-in-and-day-out discomfort that my body brings with it. That induces guilt, and it usually works. "I shouldn't be doing this," I say to myself, as I down another pill. "They've got my number. I am a weakling." And I do feel quite weak. Until the pill takes effect.

Two percent of our national population is in jail, on parole, or coming up for trial. Almost two-thirds of these persons were involved in drug-related crimes. It is agreed by all that drugs have created madness. It is a madness that has taken over the police departments, infected the legislators, rendered governors, presidents and judges plumb *loco*. They — the police, legislators, et al. — think that the way to solve the "drug crises" is by further penalties, further interdiction, further crack-downs, and further madness. They didn't learn shit from Prohibition.

In the midst of this, we genteel part-time junkies don't have a chance. Either we can go to Thailand (or any third world country) where prescription drugs are sold over the counter; or we can head out to the street — you and me and our electric wheelchairs, trying to scare up a couple of Vicodin at the corner of 4th and Broadway.

I haven't always been a junkie, mind you. Over the years, I have tried to stick with the usual legal drugs: cigarettes (fifteen years), alcohol (thirty-five years), coffee and tea (forty years) and the over-the-counter trash — aspirin, Execedrin, Vanquish, and more recently ibuprofen. I even did peyote when *it* was legal. (It was legal, for some 8,000 years — until the Food and Drug Administration and Congress decided the visions it gave us were just too dangerous. All it did for me was to make me realize that all reality is fantasy, all fantasy reality. Good thing they made it illegal. I might still be there. Besides, it didn't do diddley-squat for my aches and pains.)

Rest assured, I know all the propaganda about drugs. I know that by being a pillhead I am not facing up to my pain. I'm not being brave. Better I should go to a Pain Clinic and do auto-hypnosis and feedback, right? Once I learn to live with my agony, I can hold up my head, be proud, get on with my life (with a song in my heart and a grimace on my face.)

Unfortunately I find I can get on with my life just fine with Darvon. I have a wonderful time for the few hours after I take my drug of choice. Not only does it get rid of my nagging headaches, nagging backaches, nagging joint aches, nerves and lousy self-image — it makes me absolutely charming. Darvon mixes perfectly with the White Zinfandel I serve with my meals. During dinner, I'm regale my friends with witty and sage stories out of my past. Afterwards, my dreams are better than Disneyland (last night I dreamed I was starting a series of Savings-and-Loans around the United States. It was fun and very cheap — I had the government 100% behind me, just as in the socialist countries — and the dream only cost me seventy-five cents, that being the cost of one pill).

⧖

I don't know whether there is any solution. I'll always have to scheme to get my drugs, at least until the United States decides to enter the 20th century and stop treating us all as demented children. And I'll continue to feel guilt until they (and I) realize that the 20th century is the century of wars fought and not won. WWI led directly to WWII, which in turn led to the Korean War and the War in Viet Nam, which may have led us to the realization that there are some wars we can't win. The War on Drugs is about as successful as the Russians in Afghanistan, or that one you've been having with your mother for the last thirty years.

You and I are the victims in the propaganda against drugs. We should not and cannot enjoy ourselves (they say). It is wrong (they say). Medicine is meant solely for "pain and suffering" (they say). Any other uses will lead us deeper and deeper into the black hole of addiction, shame, misery, woe, and death.

Those of us who believe the contrary will suffer mightily. And I'm probably the prime example of that.

JERRY'S KIDS: THAT'S US!

A circle gathered around us. A fight seemed inevitable. One of the young men provoked Stilitano outright.

"If you're not a fruit, come on and fight."

Before getting to the point of fists or weapons, hoodlums gab it out for a while. It's not that they try to softpedal the conflict; rather, they work themselves up to combat. Some other Spaniards, their friends, were egging the three pimps on. Stilitano felt he was in danger. My presence no longer bothered him. He said:

"After all, boys, you're not going to fight with a cripple."

He held out his stump. But he did it with such simplicity, such sobriety, that this vile hamming, instead of disgusting me with him, ennobled him. He withdrew, not to the sound of jeers, but to a murmur expressing the discomfort of decent men discovering the misery about them. Stilitano stepped back slowly, protected by his out-stretched stump, which was placed simply in front of him. The absence of the hand was as real and effective as a royal attribute, as the hand of justice.

— *THE THIEF'S JOURNAL*
JEAN GENET

ON MY FIRST AND LAST TRIP TO Mahabalipuram, India, we made a stop-over to look at the temples, the important (and startling) Dravidian rock carvings, hundreds of years old. Just outside the temple was a Tamil riding on the back of his brother. He was in his early twenties, but because of polio, he weighed no more that eighty pounds, and his arms and legs were wound around his brother's body like a spider's. He held out one hand, asking that we give him a few piastres for his pains. If you tried to duck, or went the other way, his brother would run to get him back in front of you, ignoring that space so honored by us westerners.

I thought that because I was in a wheelchair, he would leave me alone — but I was wrong: I was at perfect eyelevel, and I remember that claw-like hand, and the beady eyes, and the cold persistence — all about an inch from my nose.

What was it that bothered me about this pushy man-on-another-man's-back? Was it the same feeling I got when I read the tale of Stilitano? Was it the lack of shame, the absence of pride, the blatant blackmail? Was it the bold use of pity to extract money? And why did it make me think of Jerry's Kids?

⧗

Most of us Crips from the 50's and 60's were trained — deeply, repeatedly — to treat what ails us as nothing special. We were taught to be cool — to pass among the Normals, to smile, to be strong and untouched (and untouchable), to ask no privileges. We defined denial as freedom. We certainly didn't want to be one of those who would whip others with their pain, allow guilt to be transformed into gilt.

Among thieves and the very poor — fundraisers all — the code is different. One uses everything one can to gain some advantage: animal force, street smarts, pity. If you are a Peruvian with a broken back, an African with the Purpa, a Moslem with leprosy — you don't hide it in the closet: you haul it out and use it as a personal welfare device. It becomes a tool for survival, for in a desperately poor society one must utilize every possible means in order to live.

The poor and the thieves — they have a different moral system than the rest of us (we like to think). They're different from us (we like to think). I wouldn't be caught dead using their tricks (we like to think).

Then along come the professional fundraisers. Jerry's Kids, the sweet smiles and clean faces used to whip us up — and to whip us — for contributions. The palsied bodies, the tears, the raw sentiment (this could happen to you!), all with the purpose of extracting millions of dollars from a willing audience. It is a highly programmed, highly organized blackmail, utilizing every device, every tool. And those of us who have lived with our disabilities for years watch, and catch ourselves thinking, "That's us on the screen — those kids, with their sweet faces, and their bodies..."

And then we think, "Those bastards are doing a number on us — all of us."

And, "The fuckers show no shame, no shame whatsoever."

We thus become doubly caught: first, by whatever it is that laid siege to our bodies; then by the image of them (us!) gracelessly paraded before the world — a guilt-provoking device, utilized for the bucks. We are doubly stuck with the very name we so often fight: victims.

⧖

People struggle not only to define themselves but to avoid being defined by others. But to be a cripple is to learn that one can be defined from outside. Our complaint against society is not that it ignores our presence but that it ignores our reality....The outline of the shadow we cast has been created not by us but by those who will find a way to see what they want to see rather than what is there.

— *FALLING INTO LIFE*
LEONARD KRIEGEL[12]

How then do we face the world that wants us not as ourselves, but as a parody? How do we handle those who want to get us in a place where they can project themselves onto (but not into) our bodies; project heroism, stick-to-itiveness, bravery; project sympathy and pity — confusing both with love and approbation; project everything but reality — never, ever the reality of it?

You and I (and Kriegel) know that we represent, in our public appearances, the truth. Like us, there is not a single one of them out there — the temporary Normals — who will not die; and as they do so, many of them will preface that dying with crutches, wheelchairs, walkers, gurneys. To watch us rolling or bumping past them is to

---

[12]North Point Press (San Francisco, 1991)

remind them of their fate, a fate they don't want, a fate they think they can, by magic, bypass.

James Baldwin once suggested that the roots of racial prejudice came from the fact that Blacks were seen as shadows. What he meant by that was that Afro-Americans, with their darker skins, become a projection field, a movie screen (if you will) for whites. Honkies are thus able to lay on Blacks their Calvinistic sins (unbridled lust, laziness, lack of responsibility). Through this process, Calvinism and Puritanism become the other face of slavery, and racial prejudice becomes the filter so that people can assign their 'darker' selves to others, get it off their own backs.

Most of us Crips resent it when they, the Normals, use our crutches and wheelchairs — our surrogate bodies — as projection devices for their own insecurities. It turns up in all the things they choose to say to us in the Post Office, on the street, in the grocery. Stories of Other Crips They Have Known, tales of imagined bravery (ours and others), or the simple, Chins-Up greeting ("You're doin' Grrreat!") Our resentment springs from the fact that we are at these times denied the chance to be ourselves. We become, as Kriegel points out, what they think we should be.

In one way or another, we have thus become Stilitano — pushing our stumps into people's faces whether we want to or not. Without meaning to, we become the Indian, riding on his brother's back, exposing his body in order to get the loot. Without any effort on our part, and despite our most heartfelt wishes — we become Jerry's Kids, crying for help, or rather, not crying: thus bravely asking for help.

We try to be cool, in our wheelchairs, trying to make it from the street to the grocery store or Post Office without hearing some stranger's case history, without being told, interminably, that "Jesus Loves You." But the truth is that we *are* Stilitano (and the Indian, and the Kids — all of them) if for no other reason than the fact that they, the Normals, see us this way, push us into that mold, make us into cripple stick figures that we may angrily reject, but are forced to live with.

Robert A. Jones, columnist for the *Los Angeles Times*, recently wrote a laudatory article about the MDA and Jerry's Kids. They do, after all (he said) raise millions of dollars for a good cause — and what difference does it make if there is a bit of mawkishness, a few tears in the process?

I wrote him a letter and said, among other things:

"The television stations involved in the Telethon garner enormous profits through the time they 'give' to charity. The MDA cleans up: their administrative costs are among the highest of the large charities (that means that relatively less money goes to research and medical care for Muscular Dystrophy, more to executive perks.)

"And The Kids? They are mannikins upon which this massive larceny is perpetuated, toys in the time-honored fantasy fund-raising world of sentiment, blackmail, crocodile tears, and whatta-pity.

"It would be funny if it weren't so exploitative. If it would help your somewhat occlusive vision, I'll be happy to introduce you to some poster kids from years ago. Ask them how much they liked their bodies being exploited for national fund raising campaigns for Easter Seals and the March of Dimes. For ten million dollars or so, they were turned into little whores. They didn't like it then; they don't like it now."

Today, I reread my letter to Jones and realized that my vituperation is of such a nature that I lost sight of the central fact of our lives (yours, mine, the Kids'). That somehow this image of us as needy but sweet-tempered basketcases may overwhelm us as individuals, but there is, in truth, little or nothing we can do about it. We are, to the world, Stouthearted — even if we just got up, had a bad breakfast, and are fretting about the kids and the mortgage. We are stuck in the mold of their vision of us, and we'll always be there, and that's it. Our rage at their twisted projections is useless.

I should have saved my effort when I wrote Jones, I thought; I should have just quoted Kriegel:

> *Nonsense does not cease being nonsense when it is cloaked in metaphysics or theology....Cripples have no choice but to attempt to establish the terms and the boundaries of their existence, and they should recognize that in choosing to do this they are going to offend those normals who have an interest in cripples remaining what they want to perceive.*

THE FROG'S GOLDEN CHARIOT

ONE TIME NOT LONG AGO JESÚS asked what it was like, the first few months, when I was a new Crip. I said, without thinking about it at all, that it was *"avergonzado."* The word means "embarrassed" or "ashamed" — but it also means "shy." I thought a bit about that. My answer, which I couldn't really explain to him, came from four decades ago. It seemed to be so different from the way I feel now.

I remember, though, that I *was* shy. I also felt nothing more or less than shame when someone would ask me "What happened to you?" Being a Crip during that first few years was just something I didn't like thinking about. It was a new feeling of a new emptiness, a strange new life cut so suddenly from the old.

By the time I got out of Rehab, all my friends had gone back to college, and — as part of my new shyness — I wasn't exactly sure I wanted to be around them anyway. There were so many things that I was not going to be doing any longer. Like going out to Mandarin, getting drunk on the way, and once there, all of us piling out of the coupe and running to the river stripping off pants and shirts as we run racing to see who would be first (our young male bodies still so new to us — and all this hair!) to fall into the cool waters drunk and giggling, spraying water at each other, roiling about in the waters like great free seals.

"I was embarrassed because now all of a sudden there were so few things I could do," I told Jesús. I had a host of new and strange feelings. One was that it was a dream, and that soon the dream would be over. Another was that some part of me felt that I had *let my friends down* by turning Crip. I could explain the first one but not the second.

> *These are things that can be no longer, I thought. The past is to be no more, I said to myself. The hope of the last few months during 'Rehab' is now to be crushed. "You will walk again, I am certain of that," my mother would say, often, too often, too blithely (I thought) — so now after the months it became no longer god's failure, but my own. These things are to be no longer.*
>
> *Regret, too, is to be tolerated no longer — nor are the memories. No longer will there be days in the sun running to the waters, god-easy in my body, arms and legs and me moving so easily, so quickly. That is to be no longer.*
>
> *With a new body and a new self, I cannot react as the sunny child from before, but with a new way to go along with a new body. It doesn't work as they want, not like before: the prince has been transformed by the kiss of fever into a frog, and the frog no longer works like a charm: it's got new funny legs and hands — seems a bit more slippery now. There will be a new self to go along with the new body.*

It was February of 1954, exactly a year and a half after the fever, and six months after I had emerged into the world from my cocoon of hospital and rehabilitation. It was suppertime, late summer, and I was sitting at the old

kitchen table in my new wheelchair, reading, always reading, and my Aunt Jane — the one who was always closest to
me as I was growing up — was cooking supper and she
didn't know that I was watching (I was supposed to be
reading) and the tears were running down her cheeks. No
one was there but us, and she imagined I couldn't see the
tears but I did. I knew she was thinking of me from the not-
too-distant past when she'd be cooking and I would be
sitting there at the table, hot and dirty, fresh in from from
play, laughing, talking with her. Only now, I wasn't in from
anything, except (only) from near-dying. And I certainly
wasn't laughing.

I could see her face reflecting that memory of me
from Before, the memory of her youngest nephew — the
wild one — now in his shiny new wheelchair, and she was
thinking, "My poor darling." (That was the phrase she had
always used with unfortunate poor, bereaved, or dying.)

The lone dinner with my Aunt Jane, she so lost over
what she lost (me) and what I lost (my past), and I knew I
had to be out of there, off away from those tears that were
killing me because tears don't work for me anymore.

*They're drowning me. I'm not ever going to 'get better'
or 'be cured' or 'walk again.' I'm only going to escape.
The death of her nephew is now complete, and if she
wants to cry over the corpse, she can — but it's another
corpse of another era, perhaps even of another person.
The boy is fled, a spirit off on its own somewhere
perhaps, wandering about, getting drunk with ghostly
pals on the beach, well away from this new body which,
ready or not, is to be Home for the rest of my days. The*

*reverse conversion: by the kiss, the beautiful prince is
transformed into the frog.*

*They can weep for the lost prince, they can
bewail his disappearance — but the frog knows better.
He knows that if they don't like frogs, that's their
problem, because he will come up with a new and
different way of moving and thinking and feeling in
this new world. He has been burned alive buried and is
now resurrected in new form, and they may mourn his
death but their tears touch only the past and have
nothing to do with the present.*

⧗

It was a yellow 1953 Pontiac coupe with new hand
controls for brake and accelerator, and it was the golden
chariot of freedom. With my chariot I could get away, it
was a magic carpet away from all that. It was a new home
away from home and with it I could cross new rivers, to
places where I had never been before, places where no ashes
would be stirred...

*...in my new chariot, there's no one with me, no one to
watch me, watch my face, see how I am reacting, to ask
me (ultimate sin) if I remember from before — trying,
perhaps, to trap me into saying that I remember and
remember that I lost something, that I feel a loss, one I
regret. There's no one in or around my golden chariot to
trap me into talking about those feelings that we must
as of this moment begin to bury.*

I drove to places I had never been before, to Live
Oak, Gainesville, St. Augustine Beach. I drove fast, too

fast, although I was good with the new hand-controls. Sometimes I drove fifty, a hundred miles, and then I just turned around and drove back the same fifty or hundred miles. It was a new freedom. I roamed the streets and highways of a new past that I created, and no-one stopped me.

I am the spirit, the ghost (the ghost past my own past). It's a new life I've been given, not the old one: it's gone. The barn is burned and I will not be sifting through the ashes any more. The barn is gone, the horses have all run away, and the night and its cradle moon from back then is none of my own. I'm off alone to a new country-side, down a new road to find new friends, new paths from a new life growing vines around me. With my new chariot of freedom I shall build a new past.

⧗

The car got me gone, made it possible for me to survive in this new environment before I escaped for good, into college, into marriage, into trying to escape from the past forever, the past that would never leave me alone.

I sold it not long after. It had done its job — to spirit me, and spirit me away. If I had any love for the past, even the recent past, I would have kept it, for it had made it possible for me to put 60,000 miles between me and Before. I had driven it blind drunk (and had survived). I had attempted my first new passion with my new love Francine while driving at 60 mph (hands on her half the time, hands on my hand controls the rest).

I had used it to to build a new way, and no one was going to make me return to the past. *If you try to get me, I'm gone* was the message, and it was a great run. The golden chariot and I ran a race from them and from me.

We created a new world together; one I knew (I thought) they would never be able to take away from me.

Only I could do that.

FOR LOVE OF THE NOISY ALCOHOLIC

I CAN ALWAYS SPOT HIM FROM A MILE off, just as he can spot me — me in my wheelchair, he walking down the street. He has that shambling gait and inflamed sense of friendliness — and the stink. The stink of old, bad booze.

Before I can do anything he is in front of me, holding out his hand to me, ready to be my friend, ready to spend the rest of the day, the rest of his life with me. "'Migo," he says loudly, very loudly. "My fren,'" he says, leaning over me, breathing on me. I wonder how I am going to get away from him. Jesús, my usually faithful attendant, has wandered off, leaving me to bask in the warm sun for a while — my attendant off somewhere, chasing some skirt down the street. And I am suddenly alone, very alone.

The boozer stands rooted before me, delighted with his find. He is an expert at spotting vulnerablity for, after all, his own vulnerability has been the key element of his life for however long he has been doing this noisy street scene. Me in my wheelchair, parked on a hilly street; and he knows (and I know, and he knows I know) there is no way in a hundred years I can get away from him. I look around for help, and everyone is looking away from us, *everyone*. They don't want to get involved.

He leans forward and for a moment I think he is going to kiss me. He doesn't, though. He just wants to look hard in my eyes with his own, reddened as they are by dozens of years of devilishly hard drinking — fighting the demons within with demon rum.

"How am I going to get out of here?" I think, and I count my resources, carefully cadged over the years. Be blasé — ignore him; involve myself in friendly — albeit distant — conversation, buying time; pretend I don't speak his language; play drunk myself.

I have a new friend. One who knows all too well that he has me.

⧗

We are trained, by ourselves, and by our society, and by all the propaganda that you and I read (and write), to be fearlessly independent.

We fight vigorously for this independence — dreaming up ways to eat, to get into and out of bed, on and off the toilet — so that we can be our own person, free of too much dependence on anyone else.

We teach ourselves elaborate techniques for moving about, getting through doors, into a car, or onto a bus, learning the thousand ways to get ourselves out of our boxes.

We teach ourselves to use what few muscles remain, teach ourselves to move from here to there with all the best we can muster. We want to be beholden to no-one.

And, if we are especially resourceful, we endeavor to do it all with a certain grace, so that they can look at us, as we do something especially difficult (getting up and down curbs, say; coming into a room full of people, smiling; being charming). We want them to say, "Why, he's scarcely crippled at all. And he seems so *cheerful*, too." That's what we want them to say, right? It's what they call "disability cool."

And what happens, as it will with the human psyche, is that we get good enough at it that we begin to believe the propaganda. "It's ability, not disability that counts." That's one of the lines they taught us. "I can do anything if I set my mind to it." That's another — good, strong, believable. "Triumph of will over body," we say, turning it into a war, ignoring the irony of the Civil War imagery. It's the euphoria of fighting a battle, with the odds against us, and winning, and being good and doing good. We have a lot of cheerleaders.

Then this dumb alcoholic comes along, just when we start to think that the battle is over and done with, and spills our cookies for us. All over the street.

⧗

They come to us in many disguises — some obvious, some not so. The noisy boozer on the street, the solemn lady on the elevator, the clerk at the store. Sometimes it's a stranger at a party, managing to say just the wrong thing at just the wrong time. "Why, what happened to *you*?" That's a hot one — especially when we've had a bad night, had trouble getting up in the morning, just wanting to get through the day as quickly as possible, making as few tracks as possible.

"I felt really bad this morning," says the pleasant-faced lady in Mervyn's. She's wearing a nice paisley dress when she stops me, so I smile up at her and nod. "I really did," she says, "and then I saw you, and I feel 100% better."

Dear Lady — she doesn't even know, not for a moment, what cruelty she speaks. Not for a moment.

We've tried the responses, all of them, but sometimes we don't want to come up with any more understanding smiles, or nods, or pleasant chit-chat. "I know what you mean." "Yes, it was forty years ago…" "It's the breaks, you know…"

Sometimes we just want to fade into the woodwork and be anonymous — be not even a Crip (that would be nice!) And then, along comes that alky. Who won't let us be still, or proud, or special. We're his mark.

⧗

The key to all this lies within. The key question is, "Why does this man make me so fearful?" Since he creates anger in me, and since all anger comes from fear — the question has to be, "Why does he make me so fearful?"

He sees my vulnerability — my inability to move quickly away from him, unlike the thousands of others on the street, he sees it, and he *uses* it. In my wheelchair, I am trapped into being with someone I don't care for, whom I will never care for, one for whom I have nothing but hate.

And how do I fight it? Give up going out in the world? Or always be surrounded by body-guards? Or, perhaps, learn to be more tolerant, more accepting, more kind, more understanding of the fools of the world. I must be kind, even to those who use me for their own ends, in their own ways.

To create love for this alky will take time, as it did with the kids. For years I couldn't stand the children, with their infernal questions, but something happened in the

last ten years (perhaps age, perhaps wisdom, perhaps toler-
ance): now I revel in the company of children, am willing to
explain to them slowly, and patiently, much of my story.

⌛

It's the guy at the Post Office who tops it. He comes
up to me, ignoring everyone else, and says, "You know,
Jesus loves you." He is talking (loudly) not to me, but to my
wheelchair. He sees me as his helpless mark. Like the alky,
he is there to poke at me not with his love but with his
needs. He's testing me. He is trying to pull me back into
that rage that ran me for a quarter-century; that made me,
in my anger, the despair of family and friends. He is trying
to make me regress to the days when I was the prototypical
Angry Crip — so angry that I didn't know how angry I was.

"You see what happens to you if you don't love Jesus
enough?" That's his unspoken message, what they call "the
unseen agenda." "If you come to Him now — you will be
walking again. Sin has crippled you." That's his message —
and why does it make me so angry? Is there a dark part of
me that buys into his cruel, un-Christlike words? Or is it
that he is trivializing so many years of angst and anguish
(and triumph) by stuffing me into his dark bag marked
"SINNER?"

"I know, I know Jesus loves me," I say, nodding, oil-
on-water, trying to smile, turning deftly to get away, almost
running over his toes with my wheelchair.

"I know he loves me," I say, "because I *am* Jesus.
And I definitely do love me."

THE LOSS OF A CHILD

I HAVE SAID REPEATEDLY TO THOSE WHO will listen (and often, to those who won't) that the main trouble with us Crips is that we are so overwhelmed with the powerful messages of our own bodies that we have trouble relating to messages sent to us by others. And those who are blessed with an energetically self-centered personality (as I am) become damn near impenetrable.

I remember when my daughter was three. One of the things they love the most at that age is to be lifted up, tossed around, held upside down. I had been away a long time. There had been other adults around her to give her this physical lift. When she ran up to me for the first time in a year — me, her real daddy — she held her arms up so I could grab her, hoist her up in the air. However, with my new crutches and my tender balance, there was no way in hell I could lift her off the ground, much less kneel down (or even lean over) and hug her. I remember her standing there before me, her arms up, for what seemed like hours.

I don't know what happened next. I may have reached down as much as I could, to pat her on the head, or run my fingers across her cheek. "Daddy, daddy," she was saying. "What the hell am I doing here?" I said to myself. "I'm no father," I said to myself. I left soon after, and never went back to her, to her mother, to their world.

I am sure there were a dozen other reasons why I left: a flagging marriage; a new world of passion so alien to that of heterosexual love; a new career. But there was that other presence: a body — my body — that bore so little relationship to the one which I had grown up in. I was, to all intents and purposes, another man.

I was not much of a presence for her over the next decade. We were reunited for a few years during her teens, but it was tense at best. We lost touch again, and I haven't heard from her for several years. I certainly haven't met her new husband. She did send me a printed notice of the birth of my grandchild. That was several years ago. Friends have visited. They tell me that my new granddaughter is very beautiful, has long silken hair like her grandmother's; eyes like glaciers, just like her mother.

⌛

Despite all the ennobling publicity we Crips get in the media, along with legislation that helps us onwards and upwards — and a new psychological thinking that is just beginning to recognize us as a separate subgroup with separate psychological problems — despite all this, I have always claimed that we pay a heavy price for our bodies. Whatever compromises or survival techniques we adopt are, for most of us, hard-fought at best, emotionally debilitating at worst. *FDR'S Splendid Deception* cites a Navy study in which it was shown that we have far higher rates of drug and alcohol abuse than the Temporarily Able-Bodied — and the figures for suicide are astronomical compared to our "normal" peers.[13] This, despite being surrounded by multitudes of professionals and institutions and therapy and support groups designed to carry us beyond our lousy self-image. One of my shrinks (I've been to twelve so far)

---

[13]See Introduction.

said that all humans have four main survival and growth systems: the intellectual, the spiritual, the emotional, and the physical. When one of those gets knocked out, that leaves you a tripod. You know how stable tripods are. When another leg goes out — well, that's us. Or at least, in certain painful periods of my life, that's been me.

⧗

As I say all this I don't want to be too discouraging. I look back on me in 1960 and realize that I was a sleepwalker (on crutches.) Back then I didn't have the methods of dealing with the world that I have now. If a three-year-old came up to me now and wanted me to pick her up, I would immediately get in my wheelchair so I could pull her up on my lap and spirit her about (they loving riding on anything with wheels — especially on daddy's lap). And I would make extra special efforts to be available to her for what she needed for all those years from age zero to fifteen. But that is all wish-and-what-if: I was — then — so blown out of my mind by my body that I could not dream of taking care of the physical and emotional needs of a growing child. After all, I could barely take care of my own physical and emotional needs. For me to return to a wheelchair for any purpose whatsoever so soon after leaving it — even to help my own daughter — would have been a step backwards and downwards.

⧗

That fear has been one of my discoveries in this journey in this new body over the last forty years. Another is that we don't lose our bodies just once, we lose them over and over. In the "normal" body — whatever that may be — there are millions and millions of extra circuits, cells, operating mechanisms that make the journey through life relatively easy. You and I have lost most of that redundancy and as we get older we lose more of what is left, and more quickly. To lose 98% or 99% of the ganglia (as I and many of my fellow polios did) means that we spend the rest of our lives trying to tease out that tiny percentage of muscle power that remains to us. Now comes Post-Polio syndrome, which means a continuing decay in whatever powers we built up years ago: powers we thought, foolishly, we would have forever.

That is one of my revelations. Two others — and two vitally important others — have to do with the place of denial and anger in the world of Crips.

Denial is one of the great face-saving elements of our lives. As Gallagher has pointed out, it made it possible for an entire country to deny that President Roosevelt was disabled; even made it possible for all of them to deny their denial. A very potent force indeed.

Then there is the anger. I have spoken before of how we Crips rail at the institutions designed to help us. We thrive on cutting remarks delivered to family or friends, with layers of sarcasm and cynicism. We brutalize ourselves — sometimes subtly, sometimes not so subtly. We put out magazines like *The Disability Rag* which are monuments to our anger at government, society, advertisers, the whole world of help-the-disabled.

The ultimate comes in the joining of the two — denial and anger. I may be furious at the world and my body in the world, but if you were to ask me why I am angry, I would not only deny the anger's existence, I would ask you where you get off pretending to be a shrink. In other words, I would be angry at you — but in a most subtle way, as if it weren't happening at all. Sarcasm is a marvelously effective distancing device — from the other person; from the self.

This brings me back to my original thesis about parenting. I suspect that most of us are probably poor risks as parents until we get to that enviable position where we know ourselves well enough not only as humans, but as Crips. Only then can we overcome whatever inner turmoil our bodies have laid on us — and become loving persons, worthwhile parents who can be good to ourselves, good to those around us, good to our children.

⌛

The last time I was with my daughter was at a wedding in the fall of 1985. One of our dumber relatives said to her, as she was standing behind my wheelchair, "Here. Push him over here so I can take his picture with the bride and groom." My daughter solemnly announced, for all to hear, "I don't push my father anywhere."

That sort of earned insight made me proud of her then — and makes me grieve doubly over the bad mix of psyche and physical loss that created our parting in the succeeding years. How I miss her, and her fine ability to see me as I really am.

LORENZO W. MILAM

III. REVIEWS

" This is what has puzzled me so about the biographies of Franklin D. Roosevelt: the man was a paraplegic, yet this important fact is given very little attention. FDR's disease and seven years of convalescence are treated as an episode in an early chapter in these books and never mentioned again. This is absurd and unreal. A visible paralytic handicap affects every relationship, alters the attitudes of others, and challenges one's self-esteem. It requires meticulous minute-by-minute monitoring and control to an extent quite unperceived and unimaginable by the able-bodied. This condition of being handicapped generates a range of emotions, whether expressed or not, that must be dealt with, not just at onset, but continuing throughout the rest of the patient's life...The central key to understanding FDR's personality and motivation — the impact of his handicap — has been all but ignored by historians..."

— *FDR'S SPLENDID DECEPTION*
HUGH GREGORY GALLAGHER

DON'T WORRY, HE WON'T GET FAR ON FOOT
The Autobiography of a Dangerous Man
John Callahan
Morrow, 1989, 219 pages.

SOME THOUGHTS ON CRIPLIT

Callahan draws a cartoon series entitled "The Lighter Side of Being Paralyzed for Life." He's thirty-eight, severed his spine seventeen years ago in an automobile accident in Long Beach. This is a tale of growing up in a supposedly normal Catholic family in the Pacific northwest. It is, too, a tale of alcoholism, carousing, The Accident, more alcoholism, more carousing, attempts to self-destruct, carousing, rehabilitation:

Since my body would now have to be hauled around, dressed, maneuvered in and out of bed, made love to and so forth without voluntary control, it would need to be capable of extraordinary flexibility. I was strapped to a tilt table, a padded board about four feet off the ground, fitted with a footrest to keep me from sliding off. A leg would be splinted and attached to a rope coming down from a pulley on the ceiling. Then the rope would be tightened and the leg pulled up as, simultaneously, the table was tilted down. A few more inches every day. If I'd been able to feel it, I would have confessed to heresy or anything else after a few seconds; instead, after an hour of this daily for six months, my hamstrings were so abnormally stretched that I could have stuffed my toes in my ears. If I could have moved them...

Callahan is a funny Crip, but like all funny people, his tales and cartoons are peppered with the truth of living with a dysfunctional body twenty-four hours a day, seven days a week, fifty-two weeks a year, on and on. Our bodies don't go away — and a good writer has to interleave humor and wit with the honest grief at what is, after all, the ultimate knowledge of the human condition.

Few authors have been able to pull it off: dark humor and cynicism tend to take over; they don't always work for the entire length of a book. The solution has to be a mix of honesty, poignancy, and black (and white) humor. At first, the black humor predominates — like this from Callahan's stay in an old people's nursing home:

> *My roommates were nearly always in the last throes. More than once I woke up in the morning and had to ring for the Cheryl on duty.*
>
> *"What do you want, Mr. Callahan," she'd ask, obviously put out.*
>
> *"Well, my roommate here seems to be history…" And sure enough, the guy would be facedown in his breakfast tray when she entered the room. "Must have been the powdered eggs," I'd grin. They'd clean him up, and the undertakers would come and take him away, making me even later for school…*

Black humor. Is that what it is? "Black?" Is that something we've recently invented — or is it right out of the heartland of English literature? Mad King Lear lurching about on the storm-swept plains, the Fool at his knees, raging at the heavens; Swift's "Modest Proposal," suggesting the Irish make pork pies out of their children, since that is what they're best at producing (children, not pies);

Defoe's careful and sometimes cruel observations of the habits of Londoners during the plague years; Faulkner's misshapen, funny Southerners — one hero a eunuch idiot; Nathanael West's girl who was born without a nose, "although my father buys me pretty dresses and tells me I can dance nice;" Nabokov's blind hero, being cuckolded by his wife and his best friend silently there before his sightless eyes.

Actually, when you think about it, all humor is black — for what is humor, after all, but the bizarre juxtaposition of things that don't belong together. In black humor, something's askew — for sure — but it's merely askew in a deadly or heartbreaking or insane way.

Callahan's situation could be described as heartbreaking — if you're into that frame of mind. The handsome, powerful young man, now in his wheelchair, a man who used to spend his summers working in the aluminum mill, going out to drink and battle with his fellow millworkers at night — now, by contrast, forced to ask someone to help him get his wheelchair out of the men's room when it gets stuck, as it often does, in one of the booths.

It could be heartbreaking, if you choose to think in that peculiar way — but that would say more about you than about Callahan because, truly, all of us are A Heartbreak — especially when we continue blindly ignoring where we have been, and where we are going. To define him as tragic loses him, and — even worse — loses *us*. Callahan merely lies at the edge of our self-definition, what Ellison called the "break point."

People sometimes say, "You have such strength and you've been through such tragedy." And I always remember the cartoon I drew years ago of an obese man who has fallen flat on his face and spilled all of his candy. He's thinking, "What kind of a God would allow a thing like this to happen?" When I think of this cartoon, I realize I don't feel sorry for myself any more.

Callahan's realization is not a perfect realization — at least not yet. He's only had seventeen years to work on his new body. He says, "I don't feel sorry for myself any more." Is he thus safely beyond misery, self-pity, the this-can't-be-me stage? Probably not. In saying "I don't feel sorry for myself any more," he's doing what the rest of us do at such times — that is, lying. The statement is denial hard at work. The truth of it lies in the anger.

Callahan's cartoons fairly crackle with rage. And anger, as a wise critic once pointed out in a review of one of my own books: anger is one of the most subtle forms of self-pity. It doesn't ruin Callahan, or his book. In the same way that denial can often be a life-saving device, self-pity can be a saving grace at certain steps in our evolution. Only the enlightened, the mountain-top Buddhas described by Peter Mathiessen ("Right. I am crippled. I can't go anywhere. Isn't it wonderful!") have managed to rise above the pity and the anger, have no need for either in order to survive the intense, horrible, funny comedy that is being human — encased in that case of blood and bone and fat and skin called body. Callahan is half-way there.

Until very recently, what the cognoscenti call "CripLit" was solely of the Amazing Comeback Through God and Hope variety. Those of us *in medias res* read it with scorn and loathed the publishing world for producing it. We wondered at the sentimental blindness of the TABS, the "temporarily able-bodied."

Standard American triumph over all things Bad and Hurtful permitted very little of the post-WWII reality school — the German, French, or Italian modernists (Günter Grass, Andre Robbe-Grillet, Curzio Malaparte.) That which did exist was slipped in over the transom in other disguises. Betty MacDonald's *The Plague and I* was comic writing (after all, she was a 'humorist,' and had made us laugh with *The Egg and I.)* There were, even so, strong undertones of despair in this tale of years in a TB hospital in the Pacific Northwest. We didn't always notice the pain because of the superhuman effort she made to hide it, to marry grief and bodily truth with wit. That made the book special.

Then, a decade ago, they published Richard Brickner's *My Second Life* — an interesting attempt to use the author's paraplegia as a metaphor for the triumph of intellect over the physical self. Here was a head with no body, he was saying — and the head was given permission to cut out the heart — to see the disaster with reasoned, Cartesian sonority. The writing was good, careful — and as cold as ice. It was as if someone had cut Brickner's nuts off. The anger was presented in round-table discussion of his physical self. It was perfect for that intellectual arty publishing of the 70s (Brickner was — and presumably still is — a member of the New York Publishing Establishment.)

Nancy Mairs' books are the 1980s equivalent. Her first one, *Plaintext* is — like his — cool and reasoned, practiced, the writing of an English teacher (that's what she does for a living):

The other day I was thinking of writing an essay on being a cripple. I was thinking hard in one of the stalls of the women's room in my office building, as I was shoving my shirt into my jeans and tugging up my zipper. Preoccupied, I flushed, picked up my book bag, took my cane down from the hook, and unlatched the door. So many movements unbalanced me, and as I pulled the door open I fell over backward, landing fully clothed on the toilet seat with my legs splayed in front of me: the old beetle-on-its-back routine. Saturday afternoon, the building deserted, I was free to laugh aloud as I wriggled back to my feet, my voice bouncing off the yellowish tiles from all directions. Had anyone been there with me, I'd have been still and faint and hot with chagrin. I decided that it was high time to write the essay.

Mairs teaches composition. She is also a student of medieval and renaissance literature. She knows words. She also knows, without denial, exactly what has happened to her, what is happening, what will happen. Critics have acclaimed her because she writes with such honesty. But there's no such thing as a free lunch — even in the honest writing sweepstakes. In her essays, there's a element of self put-down that is so potent she can't, it seems, recognize it.

I think it comes out of the style so favored for so long in intellectual America — The *New Yorker* style of distance, coolness, and artless artfulness. Since it embodies a special kind of self-deprecation, it should be perfect for us Crips, right? Yet, there is something more to it than meets the eye:

Because I hate being crippled, I sometimes hate myself for being a cripple. Over the years I have come to expect — even accept — attacks of violent self-loathing....Even with my brace I walk with a limp so pronounced that, seeing myself on the videotape of a television program on the disabled, I couldn't believe that anything but an inchworm could make progress humping along like that....I carry one arm bent in front of me, the fingers curled into a claw. My left arm and leg have wasted into pipe-stems, and I always try to keep them covered. When I think about how my body must look to others, especially to men, to whom I have been trained to display myself, I feel ludicrous, even loathesome....

After writing this about herself, Mairs tries to save it (and herself) by saying, "the self-loathing I feel is neither physically nor intellectually substantial. What I hate is not me but a disease." She is wrong. There is an unacknowledged intolerance of self here. What should be wry — The *New Yorker* called it a Jigger of Wry — is bitter and vindictive: and it is turned inward, against the self. No wonder Mairs spends a fair part of the book describing her depressions, what they have done to her, how she tries to handle them.

It is hard to trust writers who dislike their characters, and it is great art to take someone who is unlovable — and make the reader want to know more about him or her. F. Scott Fitzgerald kept us fascinated by Gatsby; even though he was a scoundrel, we loved him (or at least accepted him) because he was such a fascinating mess of contradictions, because — too — he was one of the last great romantic heroes: a Romeo displaced to West Egg.

The character that Nancy Mairs has chosen as her hero (Nancy Mairs) doesn't work for us because the author shows too much distaste for her — and her body. She falls, as so many of us fall, and rather than cry out or rage at the gods, she laughs. It sounds like what we Crips *should* do — but the laughter is brittle, too brittle. Never in Mairs' writings do we find the necessary joining of grief, rage, beauty, and wry humor — the hallmark of one who has gotten through to acceptance. A writer reaches the world not by throwing himself or herself on the ash heap and saying, "How ugly I am!" Rather, the writer must join with the readers in a community of anguish that is neither breast-beating nor a pornographic immersion in the stink. There is no room for Tiny Tim at this hotel; but there can be, as well, no room for Captain Hook.

⧖

Falling Into Life by Leonard Kriegel is another intellectual's attempt to deal with loss-of-body. Like Robert Murphy, author of *The Body Silent* (discussed further on) Kriegel is a PhD; like Nancy Mairs, his field is English Literature. And like her, he writes those icy essays.

Kriegel reports that he routinely sets tasks that would be virtually impossible for him to accomplish. For example, getting up from the ground is excruciatingly difficult for those of us who have no use of our leg muscles. Over the years, whenever Kriegel fell, he refused all help. With a great deal of puffing and sweating, he would bring himself slowly backwards, using only his crutches, into the standing position.

He speaks of the cripple who "validates his life by creating a sense of his selfhood out of physical pain," but the selfhood Kriegel has created for himself turns out to be rather a bleak one. He says, "Having already witnessed the power of chance and accident, cripples know that if the reconciliation of their needs with the world's actualities can lead to maturity, it can also lead to madness and despair and even suicide." Kriegel — cursed as he is with a fine mind and a desperate desire to overachieve — seems to be telling us, in that East Coast indirect way, that, at times, he too has contemplated suicide.

Obviously he feels the despair that all of us Crips feel. But Kriegel, like Mairs and Brickner, not only despairs of, but seems to loathe the body that chance gave him. He spends many pages telling us the things he does to gussy up what god (and the disease) gave him: he was, for awhile, a maniac for not only walking long distances on crutches, and raising himself from the floor — but for gouts of Pumping Iron at the local gym. Having done all that, he seems little satisfied with himself. Once, I made a list of the adjectives and phrases that he uses in *Falling Into Life* to describe his legs. It is a strange compilation. It includes "lifeless," "useless," "withered," "atrophied," "sticks of flesh and bone," "crippled brace bound feet" and, repeatedly, "dead."

Some readers, especially the able-bodied, would see these phrases as honest and fitting. But the rest of us, in Kriegler's shoes (so to speak) see these words, coupled with the general tone of the book, as more a despairing intellectuality.[14] For one thing, Kriegel's legs are hardly "dead," since polio affects only the anterior horn cells of the nerves (having to do with motion), leaving the posterior horn cells — feeling — intact. It's the stretching of his morbid intellectual imagination that causes him, I suspect, to view his body so viciously. At times, it borders on self-pity:

If I know where I'm going, I know even better precisely where I've been. Best of all, I know the price I have paid for being there. A man endures the disease that has shaped him, until he one day recognizes in it the source of his vanity. He can't take it, but he takes it. There was a time when I relished my ability to take it. I'm tired of that now. And I find myself wishing that taking it were easier. In such quiet surrenders do we American men call it quits with the diseases that have shaped us.

We've said before that self-pity doesn't have to be ruinous. But as used here, it is couched in pretentious understatement which lays the virus on all "American men." It is a fatigue that all of us can sympathize with — being Crip can be insufferably boring, is certainly endlessly fatiguing[15] — but as Kriegel himself says, quoting from one of his favorite books, *The Adventures of Augie March*, "And I can't take it, yet I do take it."[16]

---

[14]It's not unlike the despair of the Existentialists out of World War II, where many of them had seen, first-hand, brutality of the combatants. The civilization they valued so much had collapsed into a frenzy of murder and blood torture. It is hard for us to realize the shock at our first learning that "civilized" nations — Germany, France, Italy — could indulge in such gratuitous cruelty, as it is hard for us to accept the fact that the body can be so disloyal and cruel.

[15]One of my polio friends, when I ask him how things are going, will say, "I'm tired of being a cripple." Then, laconically, "I want to do something else."

[16]Said by Saul Bellows' character William Einhorn. Kriegel calls him a "wheelchair-doomed poolroom entrepreneur." Sic.

There is this virtue in Kriegel's work — the recognition of "taking it" (which he translates as T. S. Eliot's "our only health is the disease.") But when he says that "my virus would stimulate and irritate me for the rest of my life," we think that he has opted more for the latter than for the former.

⧗

The first book to tackle the subject of being Crip with full fury-at-loss was Ron Kovic's *Born on the Fourth of July*. It worked (if communication is our criterion) because any reader — with any brains or heart — would have to be depressed, profoundly, acutely, and morbidly, at the message of the book. Kovic gave non-Crips the opportunity to participate in the agonizing process of separation of legs, heart, and head — no less than John Howard Griffin's *Black Like Me* made it possible for 1960s liberal Americans to live some of the racism of America without actually having to be Black.

Trouble is, nowhere in Kovic's book was there humor or joy, even bitter humor-in-loss, the joy of intellectual (or cynical) understanding. *Born on the Fourth of July* was a triumph, but it was a triumph of unremitting, steaming rage. Kovic went from being a full-time Crip to being a full-time activist, merging anger at what had happened to him with the anger many of us felt at a society that would send the innocent to war. Body again became metaphor. Kovic's body chained to the fence of the defense establishment, his wheelchair — a part of his new body — tipped over and trampled on by the Los Angeles police, became our own experience of a war that should never have been. It was the first book to present the rage of a young man at being emasculated by his country. The fact that it was his own blind patriotism that led to the emasculation doubled the irony and pain of it.

⧗

All Crip books by necessity must try to sustain the tradition of the medieval Lives-Of-Saints, where exquisite pain can be transmogrified: if not into holiness, at least into wisdom. *Don't Worry He Won't Get Far on Foot* goes in this direction by moving along the fine bridge between tragedy and comedy, between a profound sense of anger and worth-lessness, and a realized sense of self-in-suffering. John Callahan is crippled — and not merely by a Volkswagon bashing him and his head into a freeway pole at ninety miles an hour, in July, 1972. He claims that being raised a Catholic — a child abandoned in the first year of his life (he was given up for adoption by his natural mother) — was profoundly crippling. His violent accident thus became the external sign of a scarring within that ran deep enough to turn him alcoholic before the age of eighteen. The accident grew out of his attempt to exorcise the sorrow of wrongful birth, and the bitterness of a wronged life.

> *At the end of one night's drinking we were crossing the railroad on our way home when Toby's manual wheel-chair got stuck in the tracks. Struggling to get loose, he fell out of the chair. He lay across the tracks like the heroine in a Dudley Doright cartoon and moaned, "Go away, man. Leave me here. It's better this way." He wasn't kidding.*

Somehow I talked him into holding on to my powered chair while I dragged him out of the right of way, and after a long struggle I freed up his wheels before the Midnight Special could flatten them.

As a hot poultice will draw the fluids of a sty or boil, being cripple draws other psychic fluids into high relief. If he were not quadriplegic, Callahan could probably have lived a relatively normal neurotic American life — smoking dope, drinking himself into night-blindness before the television set, beating himself and his family into insensibility, either physically or emotionally — the usual American methodology of dealing with frustation and loneliness and emptiness.

Being Crip, however, has removed hundreds of options from his life. He (like many of the rest of us) is forced to deal with the truth of being different in a way that can be at once more subtle, and more destructive.

One biblical phrase with special meaning for Donny and me in those days was "Be still, and know that I am God." I felt it had been driven into my heart and head with a sledgehammer. A quadriplegic cannot leap up and relieve his emotions by becoming frenetically active. I felt as if a huge hand had reached down out of the heavens and placed me firmly on my butt in a wheelchair while a voice said, "Just sit there and relax for fifty years. Don't get up, ever." The only chance of relief from grief, from anger and from resentment I had was spiritual.

A man or woman paralyzed for life as a C-5 (partial use of the hands and arms, neither feeling nor motion from the chest down) cannot be independent, no matter how powerful the will — no matter how cunning, resourceful, and charming the personality. What does it mean to be dependent on another human being? Callahan tells us in one paragraph:

For three hours every day my body was penetrated, pumped out, squeezed dry, scrubbed down, hoisted up and down and dressed to the standards of a baggy-pants comedian. Every day, as would be forever. Most of the time I was having my very pimples popped by guys I couldn't really relate to, misfits and oddballs who were all I could afford. Even the occasional friendship was soured by dependence...

"Even the occasional friendship was soured by dependence." Most Americans will not know, until they are on their death-beds, what these words mean. "Dependence" — a word so meaningless to those who can move and walk and dance and jump and play (and, most of all, most sacred of all, can jump up and run away.) It's hard to ask those around us, even those who love us, to do things for us, intimate things, over and over again. Our bodies are not our own, and this is the heart-breaker: we are stuck with not wanting to be too demanding (a form of self-pity, right?) and not wanting to inconvenience others (that's the way we were bred, right?) Even the occasional friendship: we don't want to test it with this *thing* we have, this body, this one that works differently than it's supposed to.

We are all addicts to a dream from before, a fantasy-body that we could have lived with, adorned, used *casually*.

This other body — the Now-Me — does none of these things, doesn't even *belong* to Me. Rather, it falls to the control of one who may choose to dress it badly, feed it sloppily, care for it casually, be indifferent to it. And while this "caring" is going on, what about the psyche? I may be in the hands of one who doesn't care for me at all; how do I relate to one who is taking me through the most intimate experiences of bowel and bladder? Is that person a friend, worker, casual acquaintance, or just a pair of hands out there, doing a smelly job? Can the one who does the cath be my best friend? How close can I get to one who knows me too well — knows me for better (and for worse), far more than most husbands will get to know their wives, far more than most wives will get to know their husbands? When does intimacy strangle love?

Can one ever care for me, one who is such an intimate part of this thing I cannot control, my body (as strange to me as it is now)? Can that person truly care for me? As a friend; as a lover?

The most virulent chapter of *Don't Worry* doesn't have to do with the Catholic church, or family, or the accident. It deals with with the American system of helping the poor and disabled, our system of Welfare. According to Callahan — and he knows it well — it isn't bad: it's horrible.

> *Welfare workers never return your phone calls. They are always out in the "field." Somewhere there must be a huge pasture with five thousand caseworkers down on their hands and knees, grazing. Ask a question, and you*

get no answer. Ask to speak to the supervisor, and you'll get a runaround. If you persist and actually get to speak to the supervisor, he'll give you the runaround...In Welfare, the rules change constantly. One month I am allowed to make seventy-five dollars, the next month, nothing. I must order my medical supplies once a month. Then, once every two months. Soon again, back to once a month. Recently I learned that my weekday attendant was no longer allowed to work the weekend position...Like any bureaucracy with complicated rules, Welfare constantly creates and eliminates "exceptions" to those rules. Quads often have strained kidneys and need extra protein. So an exception allowed me to keep a little more money to supplement my diet. Then came a note that the exception had been cut off retroactively. I owed Welfare for meat and cheese I'd bought with my own money and already eaten. I volunteered to come over to the office and throw up, but they wanted cash...

It is redundant to point out that Callahan is a fighter. It is also redundant to say that his fight is a good one. He happens to be in the limelight (getting this book published, with the attendant publicity) because he is an exceptionally funny cartoonist. He should never have made it in the cartoon sweepstakes. His line drawings are often gawky and hideous — but, at the same time, they are perfect examples of form fitting function: something as complicated (and deranged) as making us laugh at basketcasery succeeds because of the method by which it is delivered on the page. A good cartoon is the boiling down of hundreds of hours (or

years) of experience into a single, poignant drawing. That's
his life, that's his work, that's his art.

☒

Callahan concludes *Don't Worry* with a typical day-
in-the-life of John Callahan. In contrast to so much of the
rest of the book, it is filled with adventure, life, movement,
people, friends, and his own grand spirit of pursuit of life:

> *The land slopes downward from Portland State to the
> city center, and I really blast along. I usually have a
> wreck each day. I'll be flying down Broadway at the
> speed of light just as the offices empty out and thousands
> of young secretaries hit the street with their high heels
> clicking, everyone heading for a bus; suddenly I'll hear
> that old telltale clunk. The drive belt! Either I smash
> through a jewelry-shop window or into a small Chi-
> nese grandmother, fresh off the boat, whose first experi-
> ence of America is to be pinned to the sidewalk by a one-
> hundred-eighty pound quad in a three-hundred-fifty-
> pound wheelchair.*

It is life that keeps him (and many of the rest of us)
going. It may be misleading, even dangerous, to call it
hope. There is humor and sarcasm and despair and horror
in it, but not necessarily hope. Rather, *Don't Worry, He
Won't Get Far on Foot* has a madness — a madness that
works. It may well be the madness of Oedipus' blindness: I
will not see the hideousness of the life process at work here

because if I do, I will fall down weeping, dying, dead on the ground.[17]

It is the madness that made Callahan, for the first thirty years of his life, try to destroy himself. Having partially failed at that, it leads him now into survival in the best sense of the word — surviving by fighting and pushing and driving — like so many of us, by not giving up, by not even making surrender an option.

Those of us who are there with him have to give up at least once a day...to *not* give up. At the moment of surrender, we hand ourselves enough credit to try another day: not better, not smarter, not more wonderful — just keeping on keeping on ("And I can't take it, yet I do take it") taking ourselves beyond the cliché (and it is a cliché) that life is the mere renting of a body for so many years — then, finally, for some of us gratefully, relinquishing it, no matter how much it has been beat up, ravaged, ruined.

It is the process of seeing that life is forgiving, and in the process, forgiving ourselves: that is what makes it workable. And worthwhile.

Callahan is half-way along this track, further, for sure, than Brickner, Kriegel, Mairs. God hope that he can carry it through to its richest and most honorable conclusion.

---

[17]It was Robert Murphy who pointed out that Oedipus was one of the original proto-crips. In reaction to the soothsayer's prediction that he would kill his father, his father had him crippled. The very word "Oedipus" means "Swollen Foot" or "Gimpy."

THE BODY SILENT
Robert F. Murphy
Henry Holt, 1987, 242 pages.

BLAMING THE VICTIM

The totality of the impact of serious physical impairment on conscious thought, as well as its firm implantation in the unconscious mind, gives disability a far stronger purchase on one's sense of who and what he is than do any social roles — even key ones such as age, occupation, and ethnicity. These can be manipulated, neutralized, and suspended, and in this way can become adjusted somewhat to each other. Moreover, each role can be played before a separate audience, allowing us to lead multiple lives. One cannot, however, shelve a disability or hide it from the world. A serious disability inundates all other claims to social standing, relegating to secondary status all the attainments of life, all other social roles, even sexuality. It is not a role; it is an identity, a dominant characteristic to which all social roles must be adjusted. And just as the paralytic cannot clear his mind of his impairment, society will not let him forget it."

The Body Silent was written by Robert F. Murphy, a professor of Cultural Anthropology at Columbia. Starting in 1972 with a spasm, and blossoming in 1986 to full quadriplegia, his body has deteriorated. The cause: a tumor inside the spinal column that will ultimately reduce his body to "full quiescence."

Murphy has, like many of us, watched his body turn from being a useful, albeit ignored, tool of day-to-day living, to an instrument which has become the center of his consciousness. It's now a body that is no longer his own, that has to be cared for by others — while he watches in (what he hopes is) understanding and dispassion.

We have, thus, a scientist looking at a brand new world, a brand new body — viewing it in a professional way. And despite *The Body Silent's* being perhaps too cool, too dispassionate, too restrained — it is loaded with what they call "earned insight."

For example, listen to him discuss the strange middle-ground that the handicapped occupy in this country:

> *The long term physically impaired are neither sick nor well, neither dead nor fully alive, neither out of society nor wholly in it. We are human beings but our bodies are malfunctioning, leaving our full humanity, to some, in doubt. We are not ill, for illness is transitional to either death or recovery. Indeed, illness is a fine example of nonreligious, nonceremonial liminal[18] condition. The sick person lives in a state of social suspension until he or she gets better. The disabled spend a lifetime in a similar unsuspended state. We are neither fish nor fowl; we exist in partial isolation from society as undefined, ambiguous people....This undefined quality, an existential departure from normality, con-*

---

[18]Being "liminal" refers, for example, to coming-of-age rites in other societies. A young man or woman will be put in limbo — set apart for days or weeks, with special foods, and special restrictions. Murphy claims that the disabled in our society are liminal, but there is no exit; we are liminal for the rest of our lives. It refers to our relationship not only to our society, but, in more intense form, to our families and to ourselves.

CRIPZEN is actually:

tributes to the widespread aversion to the disabled reported by researchers.

It's fascinating: what the author reports, and what he doesn't — or won't. He claims that he has never learned to cry; he claims never to have had major anger (the disablement came on him so slowly that he was spared rage, he says.) We, those of us who have been there longer than he has, read between the lines; he tells us more, much more, than perhaps he wants. But he also tells as much as he needs to of what has happened to his body, and what he thinks has happened to his mind and his perspective.

We are given here a fine representation of The World of the Newly Handicapped. That world is put in appropriate cultural and anthropological perspective. Old experiences come to be cast in new light, with rich, new meanings, as if someone has turned on the light in what we thought to be an empty room:

> *Quadriplegics cannot stalk off in high (or low) dudgeon, nor can they even use body language. To make matters worse, as the price for normal relations, they must comfort others about their condition. They cannot show fear, sorrow, depression, sexuality, or anger, for this disturbs the able-bodied. The unsound of limb are permitted only to laugh. The rest of the emotions, including anger and the expression of hostility, must be bottled up, repressed, and allowed to simmer or be released in the backstage area of the home. This is where I let loose most of the day's frustrations and irritations, much to Yolanda's [his wife's] chagrin. But I never vent to her the full despair and foreboding I sometimes feel, and rarely even express it to myself. As for the rest of the*

world, I must sustain their faith in their own immu-
nity by looking resolutely cheery. Have a nice day!

Because of powerful medical intervention techniques, used on so many of us to extend the term of our
lives, a great number of people in America will come willy-
nilly into the experience of being handicapped. So many
people, now out and about and walking (on what Murphy
calls "the stairs and sidewalks made by and for people with
two functioning legs") will get to learn about a new body
that works with severe limits, if at all. They will, so many of
them (50,000,000 in the next twenty-five years alone)
come to have a chance to taste sheer animal frustration, and
aching rage (what I like to call The Brood; what Murphy
calls "a metaphor for the human condition.")

They will, all of them, learn the lesson of not being
able to escape. For better or worse, they will have the
experience of having their thoughts turn and turn inside,
inescapable thoughts that come to us all — even the most
psychologically adjusted of us — thoughts born of isolation
and frustration. Fifty million people with a new knowledge
of anger and of depression, gift that keeps on giving,
merged with down-home, flat-out guilt.

> *It must be said again that feelings of guilt permeate,*
> *and sometimes bury, the families of the disabled. There*
> *is the basic, self-accusatory guilt of the impaired person,*
> *exacerbated by his or her guilt over being a burden. The*
> *able-bodied family members, for their part, feel guilty*
> *because they are intact and the other person is not. This*

may sound familiar, for all families are guilt networks;
it is at once a source of both unity and dissension within
them. But the guilts are far more intense in families
visited by disability and, correspondingly, much more
difficult to contain.

I was trying to explain to a non-Crip friend of mine about this guilt, and its first cousin — or bastard stepchild — anger. I realized as I told my story that there was no way I can convey the caustic acidity of it: what it does to those to whom we direct it and, most of all, what it does to the gentle parts of us, its progenitors. As a doubly delicious irony, I tried to explain that most every Crip I have met or spent time with, laughed and talked with, has capped his or her *parfait* of rage with the ultimate Cherry: a hugh dollop of denial — direct, or indirect. No, we say, there is no residue of choler. Yes, we manage it all with good will and cheer. Yes, all our friends and family accept and love us, with or without braces, wheelchair, the strange tilt of head or aimless movement of the hands.

I hear us say this, and at the same time, in our language and actions (often in our eyes) I see such a burning animal pissed-offedness that I want to duck out of the way so I won't get singed by it. I recognize it easily, so easily — because in their eyes I am seeing the mirror of my own imperfectly hidden pissed-offedness. Boswell called Johnson's melancholia "The Malady of the English;" and I believe that denial and forced cheerfulness is "The Malady of the Crip."

At those times we must acknowledge the singular truth so eloquently expressed by Freud, Jung, Adler, Erickson, Bowen, and their followers: that denial feeds on itself, that it begets denial; that the best way to support a case of hiding the truth is to hide even the most evanescent acknowledgement of its existence. "Who me? Angry? Perish the thought," he says, and then a moment later, he curses bitterly, with heart-wrenching vehemence, the day that he wrecked the plane, the day he neglected to go to the doctor; she speaks with singular pointedness of the Sunday when she woke with the burning fever and her family thought it was the flu, so she didn't get to the hospital until two weeks later. "Sure, I've really come to terms with it," she says, with that funny fire in the eyes. Denial of denial — one of the great forces of survival.[19]

Murphy has been twice trained. He studied at Columbia to be a crackerjack anthropologist, spent his days of field work in the jungles of the Amazon, with the Mundurucu. With his wife, he investigated the social, cultural, and interactive life of a tribe of Indians two days away, by canoe, from any civilization.

More recently, he enrolled in this other school, starting in the early 1970s, when his body began to fail him. Extensive testing, and several operations, proved that he had a spinal tumor, and that, ultimately, he would be what is called a "total." This is his secondary preparatory school, and he works with this new material in as careful and scholarly a way as he did the Indians of Brazil:

---

[19]It reminds me of one of the characters — a seventy-year-old mother named Kunti — in Peter Brook's *Mahabharata*. She has spent most of her life seeking the killer of her son. When they ask her why she looks half her age, she says, "It is anger keeps me young."

The study of paralysis is a splendid arena for viewing this struggle of the individual against society, for the disabled are not a breed apart but a metaphor for the human condition. The disabled represent humanity reduced to its bare essentials...I would lie in my hospital bed and think, too weak to concentrate on reading and yet not sick enough to watch television. And what I mused upon was myself and my new and permanently altered feelings of who and what I was. Gradually, my thoughts became disembodied, and I began to think of myself as if a part of me were perched over the headboard, watching the rest; it was as if it were happening to somebody else. Worry and foreboding were displaced in my reveries by absorption, and I became mesmerized by the magnitude of my disaster and a growing sense that it followed some deeper rhythm. And it is of this tempo, this structure, that I write.

"My new and permanently altered feelings of who and what I was..." Murphy was well past his fiftieth year when he began to experience the truth of his own mortality. He has thus had the opportunity of watching himself turn into something quite different from the active anthropologist, author of several books, Chairman of his department at Columbia, a scholar respected in his field. He has had the chance to turn inward, to view scientifically the change that occurs within. He has a chance to observe the effect of body on mind. He has been there willy-nilly while he and his friends and colleagues experience a wholly new physical self. (Indeed, some of his friends and colleagues fall away, cannot stand the guilt, or their own mixed feelings. It's hard for them, they report to him, to look at a new Murphy, now walking with a cane; later in a wheelchair; and finally, mostly abed, not leaving his house at all.)

It is not just a new Robert Murphy with colleagues and acquaintances. There is his family, his son and his wife Yolanda:

Each family is a kind of secret society, a closed universe of information and dependencies, and also of loves, hates, suspicions, and jealousies. Social relations within its precincts are charged with an ambivalence that commonly is magnified by physical handicap, and the hurts inflicted in the family are felt more deeply than any others. Distortion of interaction of the disabled with family members may be less frequent than with strangers, but it is far more pervasive and damaging, for it infects the very haven to which most people return for support, protection, and love.

Not only has his "haven" been "infected," there are staggering new feelings to deal with. Guilt, shame, helplessness — and, he says, a powerful desire to be done with it, to murder oneself, to commit suicide. And — equally as damaging — the eternal what-ever-did-I-do-to-deserve-this:

Shame and guilt are one in that both lower self-esteem and undercut the facade of dignity we present to the world. Moreover, in our culture they tend to stimulate each other. The usual formula is that a wrongful act leads to a guilty conscience; if the guilt becomes publicly known, then shame must be added to the sequence, followed by punishment. There is then a causal chain that goes from wrongful act to guilt to shame to punish-

ment. A fascinating aspect of disability is that it diametrically and completely reverses this progression, while preserving every step. The sequence of the person damaged in body goes from punishment (the impairment) to shame to guilt and, finally, to the crime. This is not a real crime but a self-delusion that lurks in our fears and fantasies, in the haunting, never-articulated question: what did I do to deserve this?

The Body Silent tells us of other losses, beyond the loss of motion. As Murphy learns the secret of insurmountable stairs and curbs — there are even humps in the floor of his house which impede the movement of his wheelchair — he also learns the restriction on honest expression which infects us, because of interior restrictions, because of restrictions of society. He suggests that we lose freedom of movement, and, at the same time, we lose the freedom to be natural.

The seriously disabled face a curious dilemma. If they wish to relate to the able-bodied, they have to be stoical and uncomplaining; anything else drives the others away. But this often leads people to look on the disabled person as a hero, which is an embarrassment, imposing great strain and added ambivalence on social ties. I am not at all courageous — rather, I am a survivor, along with a good part of my generation. I have fought off canonization over the years because, despite its charms, I know that sacred people are treated with social dis-

tance, which would join forces with the impulse to avoid the disabled and isolate me further.

Murphy has brought us a fresh and honest look at what we are, even though there is an innocence of the ultimate truths that we have to live with, that he himself is going to be forced to live with. As an example, Murphy's own life situation sounds somewhat skewed. Despite a good income, both from his appointment at Columbia and royalties on his textbooks on cultural anthropology, despite the income from his wife's work at a nearby university — he reveals the fact that he has no helpers of any sort outside of son and wife. It's a strange pride that puts the effort of lifting, moving, cooking, cleaning, getting put to bed, getting up, solely on the backs of his family. It sounds so familiar: that distrust that most of us have about bringing in strangers to work with us, to help us with our most intimate needs. We penalize our relatives with our intense sense of pride and determination and independence. Perhaps that is the subject of a whole different book: the anthropology of the disabled family. For all of us, learning to put ourselves in the hands of strangers who become intimates with our bodies means coming to terms with what we need and who we need (and want not to need at all). Yet we must do it to protect our families from the *overload* of us.

In *The Body Silent* we watch a brilliant mind learning what one of my favorite authors termed "the powerful lesson of bowel and bladder, the secret of withered arm and leg." And Murphy's prose style is equal to the task he has set for himself: that is, to provide us with a tempered story of one who is coming, as much as one can (so quickly!) to learn the truth of this poorly functioning machine,

Paralysis sets in motion a process of estrangement from others, from one's own body, and ultimately from one's self. It is a metaphor of death and a commentary on life....The disabled represent humanity reduced to its bare essentials, making them wonderful subjects for anthropological research ... Like Levi-Strauss's Indians, the paralyzed are "marginal" people, and the study of their tenuous position at the edge of society will tell us much about all of social life.

Murphy's insights are profound, and profoundly helpful for those of us who have journeyed with him: our families are not only "guilt networks," but profoundly altered by disease ("a conversation in the kitchen could be finished by the time I got there"); the disabled have so few resources that we must seek change and acceptance by "moral coercion" and we must get standing in the society "by the cultivation of admiration;" our sense of life must be brought totally within, into the brain, where, he says at one point, "I now reside;" most of us will deal with a hostile environment (the world) by staying at home, or by finding new friends among people of lower social standing who may have less sophistication but who have the advantage of more physical force (and, perhaps, passion). These are profound insights, wrought by experience well tempered in the secret oven of despair.

Murphy's is a microscopic view of physical loss, and society's reaction to such a state of affairs. Even though the facts are carefully given, the heart is carefully by-passed. But what saves it (and us) is the delicate scientific tone. This makes it less offensive, and more believable, as a reasoned examination of the disorder of the Crip world.

Unlike other writers I have read, Murphy doesn't need to sacrifice himself and vulgarize his new body in order to present the portrait of author as accepting but bitter victim.

Indeed, it may be a murder mystery Murphy is presenting us with. One with many detectives, few suspects, and two bodies.

And one of those is very, very silent.

MORE THAN AN AVERAGE GUY
The True Story of a Cerebral Palsy Victim
Who Triumphs Over His Disability
Janet Kastner
Darling Publishing, 1989, 232 pages.

THE DOUBLE BIND DEPARTMENT

It is now recognized that there are many varieties of child-abuse. Most of us are familiar with the physical ones. Less understood, and only recently described, are emotional abuses.

For example, a common psychic bonding system is described by family therapist Murray Bowen. It has to do with "enmeshment." An apparently normal family will be tied up in each other in an unbreakable way, utilizing guilt, pity, self-pity, martyrdom. Escape is difficult. A double bind is laid on any of the members who want out.[20]

Another double bind, just as powerful, just as explosive, has to do with faith. Or, perhaps better said, man's interpretation of the divine will. This is described, with exactitude in *More Than an Average Guy*, the story of Larry Patton.

Larry was born with Cerebral Palsy, and *More Than an Average Guy* describes his birth and childhood, his schooling and social life. It also tells of his parents' extensive efforts to find a cure.

Now, in "finding a cure," there has to be a built-in paradox. Are the parents being good parents by trying to

---

[20]A typical "double bind" statement made to an teen-age person would be, "Now don't start talking about moving out. [Pause]. You know how much we love you. [Pause]. If you leave, you know it would kill your Mom."

help the child triumph by any means available? Or do they, in the process, reject the truth of their child's disability? And by constantly saying, "You'll get better," do they imply that by not getting better the child is doing something wrong?

More Than an Average Guy describes Larry's life during — and after — this massive search for cure. It details the complexities of growing up in a world where one is considered "different." He is a boy who walks awkwardly — at least when viewed by the Able-Bodied. When he's excited, he flails about wildly, his voice turning incoherent. And on occasion, without warning, he falls down, at the most vulnerable times (at school, at play, on the street).

The trips to the many doctors' offices don't work. There is no miracle medical cure. The family starts seeking a miracle god-driven cure. They take Larry to prayer meetings — including several with the Katherine Kuhlman, "a woman with a widely known healing ministry."

> *At the Kuhlman service at the Shrine Auditorium, they heard the testimony of a young man who had been instananeously healed of CP two months earlier. Sitting in the audience in a complete body brace, this young man had felt as though someone had placed hands on his head and was praying for him. He felt the heat go down through his whole body, he said, and he knew instantly that he had been healed. He tried to get people to remove his body brace, but, oddly enough in those circumstances, no one would. So he went on home, removed it himself, and confirmed what he already knew. His body was perfectly controlled and no longer distorted...*

A young man cured of the exact same disease Larry has — and cured so miraculously that the people around him didn't even want to believe it (he had to go home and remove the brace himself).

For Larry's family, the moment of truth comes at the next prayer meeting:

> *The last night of the conference, they attended their second Kuhlman service of healing. Their anticipation for Larry was intense. Mrs. Kuhlman began her prayers for God's healing power to touch people in the arena...This might be the moment of Larry's healing...*

I know I'm a Christian, Larry thought. This is going to be it.

> *Nothing happened.*
> *Here I am, Lord. Come on!*
> *He knew he hadn't been healed.*

What went wrong? he wondered. Why didn't it happen?

> *"Mom, why didn't it happen to me?" he asked later that night.*

And Mum replies to her son, a son born with Cerebral Palsy, living with it, day-in, day-out, for thirteen years, desperately wanting, as we know he wants — as we all have to want, at some time — to be free, to be done with it:

> *"Don't be discouraged, Larry. The Lord knows what's best for you. Remember? He has a perfect plan for your life. And he has a place and a time for your healing."*

And Larry just sits there like a bump on a log, as he has since 1956, with his CP — sitting in what the authors so blatantly refer to as "his distorted body." "Why didn't it happen to me?" he asks his mother. And the perfect twist of the knife — the ultimate double bind: "The Lord knows what's best for you...He has a perfect plan for your life..." Translation: *Just forget all that anticipation we set you up with, Larry. Something screwed up. You don't know what it is yet (you're too young). It's Part of the Greater Plan. You'll figure out about it someday. Maybe.*

⧗

They say that Larry, now thirty-four, does systems engineering for IBM. In the Afterword to *More Than an Average Guy*, Josh McDowell of the Campus Crusade of Christ says that Larry often goes out on cruise ships, doing "a speaking ministry called Hurdling Handicaps." McDowell says that Larry's story will cause you "to hurdle your handicap." He doesn't specify which handicap he's talking about, though. It might be being born with CP. Or, perhaps, something worse. That is, growing up with a family who sticks it to their child at his most vulnerable time, in a most cruel way. All in the name of God's Love.

We don't know, from reading this book, the ultimate effect of the family's triple whammy on Larry. We find it significant that he didn't write his own story. There's a pair of discarded children's braces (well used) shown on the cover. From the blurry pictures of Larry (there are over fifty of them) it's hard to see any scars, even though you-know-who didn't miss a trick in the Double Bind Department.

Well, maybe one.

FDR'S SPLENDID DECEPTION
Hugh Gregory Gallagher
Dodd Mead, 1985, 250 pages.

CELIBATE POLITICS

Starting with his campaigns for governor of New York State, and throughout his presidency — Franklin Delano Roosevelt hid his disability from the world. As historian Hugh Gallagher says in the introduction to this book — Roosevelt was the only person in the recorded history of mankind who was chosen as a leader by his people even though he could not walk or stand without help.

Why did Roosevelt make such a massive effort to disguise the full nature of his disability? Gallagher suggests the country and the world were not ready to accept their leader as a man who could not move about on his own. We want our political heroes to be giants in every way.

Did it make any difference, and does it make any difference? The answer is yes, if we are to accept the second of Gallagher's premises. That is — the deception practiced on the American people cost Roosevelt dearly. He had to pretend he was a physically active political leader. He had to pretend he was something that he wasn't. The result — as is the case with any deep lie — was denial, depression, breakdown. Gallagher proves, at least to this reader's satisfaction, that the last eighteen month stretch of FDR's presidency was one of bare survival: a depressed man fighting to survive his own "splendid deception."

It's a fascinating book because it gives us a perspective on Roosevelt never before broadcast. We are, says

Gallagher, still living under the onus of the lie: no one remembers FDR as severely handicapped. One of the shocks of the book is the photographs unearthed by the author showing the president in his wheelchair, or on crutches. For as Roosevelt (and his advisors, the Secret Service, and his family) became more adept at "the deception" — the president moved about in public in such a way as to fool all but the closest observers. Streets and walkways were raised as ramps so that he could be driven to his destination without having to use stairs (FDR couldn't climb stairs alone). When visitors came for state dinners, or when they were taken to his office, the president would already be seated before they arrived. He would certainly never appear before them in his wheelchair. And for photographers:

> FDR has made it a rule...that photographers were not to take pictures of him looking crippled or helpless. His actual words, said to some newsreel cameramen taking his picture as he was being helped out of a car in 1928 were, 'No movies of me getting out of the machine, boys.' And from then on, remarkably, no such pictures were taken. It was an unspoken code, honored by the White House photography corps. If, as happened once or twice, one of its members sought to violate it and try to sneak a picture of the President in his chair, one or another of the older photographers would 'accidentally' knock the camera to the ground or otherwise block the picture.

Such censorship was not limited to the reporters:

> Should the President himself notice someone in the

crowd violating the interdiction, he would point out the offender and the Secret Service would move in, seize the camera, and expose the film...

Gallagher points out that the denial of FDR's handicap was not just limited to the press or the political parties — even the Republicans bought the lie — but was a mass denial, agreed to by a whole nation:

Roosevelt was undeniably and obviously a crippled man. Literally millions of people saw him moving down his railroad ramp, bent over like a praying mantis, or hobbling painfully slowly on the arm of his son. Cripple or not, the nation wanted this man, with all his magnificent qualities, as its leader. So an agreement was struck: the existence of FDR's handicap would simply be denied by all...

⧗

There are many parts of this book that are moving, unforgettable, beautifully wrought. After all, Gallagher, as a polio himself, is party to the grief, the anxiety, the necessary deception, the necessary manipulation practiced by all the handicapped, including false cheerfulness, the attempt to set others at ease, the need to appear at ease, relaxed, unconscious of a difference in physical mobility and appearance. The pressure on one who maintains this facade is real, and encumbering. As one of my totally paralyzed friends said: "There is so much cant between the world of the handicapped and the world of the non-handicapped. They are always saying how courageous we are. I hate that. I am not courageous. I am surviving. To say that a handicapped person is courageous is like saying that a black person has natural rhythm…"

The emotions and the mental set of FDR were created by the central experience of waking up one day with a fever that came like the holocaust, and left a vigorous man moveless. Every step of this growth and change and denial is outlined in *FDR's Splendid Deception.* It's a work filled with what can be called 'earned insight.' All the strategies are outlined: the methodology that was used to keep Roosevelt's visitors, the public, the congressmen in the dark as to the degree of the paralysis. At times, FDR had to be moved by hand; here was a 180 pound man, commander-in-chief of the military, who was transported bodily (in others' arms) onto and off of his beloved Navy vessels. John Gunther said, "The shock was greatest of all when he was carried; he seemed, for one thing, very small."

Gallagher's book is filled with the details of how the president was, for example, dressed for public occasions (special consideration had to be made for his braces); how his wheelchair was constructed; how the cars were equipped. Then there is the painfully worked out system to have FDR appear to walk down the convention hall aisle to the podium, using only a cane and left arm of his son. Once he got to the steps at the base of the podium, his lieutenants would come together and lift him, still apparently standing, up the stairs. They made it seem as he was floating up the stairs quite naturally.

When FDR (like any handicapped person) was in a room, he stayed in one place, did not walk about, used other people's arms and legs for his own. He had to stay seated, get things done, and do it all most charmingly, with what they have come to call "handicap cool." He was the Master.

Finally, there is a tragic — tragic in retrospect — description of how a dying president was made to appear lively and vigorous for the 1944 campaign. The deception had gone on for so long that the transition to this last (and most reprehensible) lie was easy. Out of this lie — like Yeats' "shudder in the loins" — grew Yalta, the presidency of Harry Truman, Hiroshima. What would have happened, we wonder, if they hadn't lied: if they had not taken a tottering, prematurely old, deeply depressed president, and carried him — with his full acquiescence — into his fourth, and fatal, term.

⌛

This is not only a book about the psychology and *modus operandi* of the handicapped; it is not only a specialized history, one dealing with the handicapped and America and the presidency; it is a historical perspective on what, sixty or seventy years ago, people did to and thought about the crippled. For example, here's a description of rehabilitation facilities in the United States before the coming of Roosevelt:

These hospitals were often grim, depressing places — dark, gray piles indistinguishable from prisons and asylums. They had names such as House of St. Giles the Cripple, Children's House of the Home for Incurables, and the New York Society for the Relief of the Ruptured and Crippled. Treatment was spartan and severe...In a very real although subconsciously motivated sense, the handicapped were viewed as flawed in moral character as well as in body. The physical handicap was, as it

*were, an outward sign of some inner weakness. It was
widely held that treatment, to be effective, must have a
punitive quality to it...*

Roosevelt did not merely have to overcome his own
body's paralysis; he had to overcome a nation's paralysis in
attitude towards the handicapped. He did this in a very
Rooseveltian way: he constructed his own system; he built,
from scratch, an original and daring rehabilitation institute
at Warm Springs, Georgia. And, according to Gallagher,
not only did FDR build the institute — he helped to shape
American rehabilitation principles "into a coherent theory."

Warm Springs was the center and the heart of Roosevelt's own rehabilitation — but was, as well, the center in
the United States where polios could come for resourceful,
quality care: a place of noble architecture (often sketched
out by Roosevelt with the completing of details by architect
Henry Toombs), with, in addition, a generous and demo-
cratic attitude where staff were to be on equal footing with
the patients (who were never to be called 'patients' — at
least, not in the early days). It was simply the best rehabilita-
tive care center in the world.

One of Gallagher's theses is that what FDR did at
Warm Springs would later be carried on into the New Deal.
Rather than building on old institutions, he created new
ones. Then, too, there was the split of responsibility so that
the medical help and the patients cooperated in what was,
after all, the raison d'etre of Warm Springs — making it
possible for people to function independently, with dignity.
Too, the idea that 'treatment' should be conceived and
carried out in a humane way — with much laughter and joy
to go along with the commitment and hard work. Most of

all, the belief that people can be responsible for their own rehabilitation: not to be waited on or served or talked down to by "experts" — to be responsible for their own reentry into the world.

This book should be read by anyone with concern for the handicapped and interest in the life and times of Roosevelt. But there is one point in the book which is somewhat troubling. Amidst all the rich insight about how Roosevelt (and the country) were formed by his handicap, there appears a chapter called "Sex." Now, I am as willing as anyone to give a whirl to understanding that act of men (including FDR) which is, after all, our second most private. Indeed, one expects a vigorous man like Roosevelt, a man with such charm and strength, to be a powerful magnet for the ladies of his time. Because of the nature of polio — where sensual feeling after the illness may be heightened by the general sensitivity of the body — one would expect FDR to be as vigorously experimental in sexuality as he was in politics, economics, and rehabilitation.

Not so, according to Gallagher. It is his representation that with the trauma in 1919 of the Lucy Mercer affair, Eleanor had demanded no further physical entanglements as the price for her staying on as wife. He claims that such was FDR's ambition that he never violated this agreement; that he was celibate, The Pope President, if you will:

Franklin D. Roosevelt appears to have been celibate from the age of thirty-six until his death twenty-seven years later. This is an important aspect of FDR that should not be ignored. This celibacy was due in part, but only in part, to his handicap...Although the evidence is not overwhelming in support of FDR's celibacy

it is at least significant that there is no piece of evidence,
large or small, which counters such a conclusion...

Bosh.

One of the problems on speculating about anyone's
sexuality is that, given our society, and given the times
(Roosevelt's time being the sunset of Victorianism) one can
know so little — so very little — about one man's passion,
even as public a man as Roosevelt. Who will tell? FDR
himself did not leave any personal diaries about his lust.
His family and friends (and even the reporters and valets
and aides) were, and still are — those who survive —
extremely loyal, and silent. After all, as Gallagher points
out, Roosevelt was a captivating man — and the people
surrounding him were captivated entire, especially when it
came to keeping his bedroom secrets.

It was a time of greater discretion than now. It was a
time when the body was considered to be shameful; and the
normal love functions amongst the crippled were considered to be even more shameful. We are dealing with a man
whose friends would defend his secrets far beyond his
death. Yet out of this vacuum of information the author
purports to tell us that the active, the charming, the driven,
the obviously very virile president was a celibate.

Who knows? Who is to ever know? Is it important?
I think not. We should be satisfied that Hugh Gallagher
has constructed a book with stunning ideas, rich details,
immensely challenging thoughts — and not only with
regards to FDR as a man, as a politician, and as a hero to the
nation, but with regards to the role of all handicaps in the
life of a nation.

COLD WATER
IN WARM SPRINGS

MY FRIEND HUGH GALLAGHER HAS
been invited to Georgia Warm Springs Foundation to give a brief speech and introduce his
book on Roosevelt. It is the 40th anniversary of FDR's
death. I am offered the chance to tag along, and I do.

Our first night, we stay up late — too late for us old
geezers — geezing about on the colonnade. About us are
the hundred or so acres that FDR bought sixty years ago. It
is here that he had constructed the most magnificent of
rehabilitation facilities in the United States.

Where we sit, we can see the shadows of a dozen
long-leaf pine, hear the night sounds and a thousand thousand crickets singing masterfully off-key. The five cluster
lights bathe the campus, and us, in a creamy light. Shadows
of people long gone, friends long gone, appear and reappear
in the darkness. We are haunted with gentle memories of
this gentle place.

There is a peace here unlike anywhere else on the
continent. No — that's not true. One time, many years ago,
I was camping in Canada, on an island north of the Straits
of Juan de Fuca. But that was a harsh peace: the stars so
bright that they lit the sky, penetrating the black with a
painful needling. The peace here is more gentle. The
campus is exactly as Roosevelt designed it. They've ruined
almost everything else about the Foundation, but they've
not wrecked the peace, and the architectural dream that
Roosevelt established here.

Hugh and I were here in 1952. Significant: we never go back to our various college campuses for reunions, but religiously, once a year — usually in the spring — we make our way to Warm Springs, to sit about, to remember the old days, complain about the new. We talk about the two or three dozen friends who, like us, had escaped from dark little hospitals around the country — who were allowed to come here to revel in the expert medical care, and delicious food, and sense of vision that Warm Springs had, a vision that none of those other places had the imagination to incorporate into their tiny, medically oriented world. We can never forget that Georgia Warm Springs Foundation was set up by a politician and a member of the landed gentry; it was certainly not created by pale, thick-eyed, arrogant physicians. Doc Roosevelt: the master builder and visionary.

Those of us who have spent time here think of him in terms of The Foundation, rehabilitation, the joy of this place. We don't think of him in terms of New Deal. What's that? Roosevelt's twelve years in office were nothing compared to the twenty years he lavished on Warm Springs. And now, in the hands of his heirs and assigns — we are beginning to think neither country nor Foundation are faring all that well.

⧗

In some ways, Warm Springs never changes. But you have to do some work to find the right memories. For instance, all the buildings here were designed to be cool in summer. They didn't have air-conditioning back then; all were designed (courtyards, fountains, expansive doors and windows, extensive beds of trees) so that one could be comfortable in the fresh summer air of the Georgia hills, coming across and through the long, narrow buildings.

Well, somewhere along the line, a dozen or so years ago, some functionary thought "This will never do. Everyone in Georgia needs air conditioning." So at the usual great trouble, time, and expense, they installed noisy pumping droning machines everywhere. Which means that if you want to enjoy the breezes and the healthy airs from outside, you have to turn off the air conditioner in your room and wrestle with a variety of locks and switches and knobs to get the window open. If you are a true North Georgia Night Sound fanatic, it's worth it — except that you have to listen to the drone of everyone else's air-conditioner all night long.

You lie perfectly still in the night, bathed in the soft air of North Georgia, listening to the freight train rumbling and whistling its way through the town of Warm Springs, rattling the windows half-a-mile east of here, then rumbling off (sound mixing with the sounds of crickets) to the south, taking our hearts and our memories with it. And when the morning comes (and the morning light has an especial peach color seen no where else), the jays come to wake you: the eastern jays being so especially raucous. "Kaaah, kaaah" they screech, racing from pine-top to pine-top.

Sometimes the wind from the east leans in, coming in from the coast two hundred miles to the east, and the trees roll and sigh, reminding you of the old men over there in the village, sitting on the benches, in front of the stores, sighing, as the waitress from the local cafe strolls by, her thighs so big and strong they threaten to snap through the purple of her tight pants, and the old geezers like the trees roll and sigh, remembering when they were young, they were so full of vinegar they'd go after her in a minute, fight each other over her if they had half-a-mind. And now she's gone, and their joints hurt too much, and what's left are the old trees swaying and sighing with the winds come upland two hundred miles up from the Atlantic, from the swamp and loblolly pine country out there near Savannah, the swamp country of the Okefenokee two hundred miles to the east of here.

This is our home, our college. This is where we grew up, Hugh and I and the friends we still keep contact with, friends who were here in the last days of polio, before they found The Cure. It was here we learned to sit up and talk and feed ourselves and move about on our own. It was here that we graduated from being in terminal bed-rest; it was here we graduated into being human, independent, alive again. That's why — that must be why — we come back here again and again: this was our real graduation. Those documents they gave us at the end of our college studies were to commemorate what they had stuck in our heads. Here — no diploma; yet we come back once each year to celebrate what they taught us to do with our bodies; the grace and beauty and style of it all.

⧗

The Little White House was FDR's retreat from Washington, his wife, his mother, politics. He came here to be with his own — the patients for whom this, too, was their second home. Here he did not have to be ashamed of his wheelchair. Here there was no "upstairs" or "downstairs" to harass him, as they had been harassing him and all the rest of us for these many years.

It's a simple house, living-room with fireplace, kitchen with four-legged stove, garage with his 1930 Ford with special hand controls. There's a porch out front, over-looking Pine Mountain. There are two bedrooms, one for FDR, the other for Missy LeHand who some say was mistress, who others say was just a devoted friend. It was here — at this White House, the other White House — that FDR was truly at home. It was here that he lived in his body without shame; it was here he died.

Today, Forty Year ceremonies are to be given in front of the Little White House. There are folding chairs out on the lawn, with, perhaps, a hundred visitors, and a scattering of us old polios, there for the festivities. The podium is heavy with microphones: the television stations and networks are here. There are to be invocations, speeches, and military salutes.

The air is strictly Georgia, the skies and trees and grounds are filled with wildlife. The U. S. Marine Corps (West Georgia Branch) presents arms and colors, and "The Star Spangled Banner" is played wonderfully off-key.

We hear the invocation, and then Hugh gives his speech. He is in his wheelchair, and since all the TV microphones are way up there on the podium, and since he's too far away to be heard — his short message — so pithy, so right, is totally ignored by the television reporters.

"Roosevelt's achievement was great," says Gallagher, "all the greater because it was achieved from a wheelchair. The simple truth is that, in all the recorded history of mankind, Franklin Roosevelt is the only man ever chosen to lead his nation who could neither walk nor stand alone.

"Today, Roosevelt is an American hero, he is a world hero — but he is also a paraplegic hero. He is one of us. We do not want the nation or the world to ever forget this fact: The greatest world hero of the 20th century is a paraplegic in a wheelchair..."

The newsmen are talking among themselves. This is not their meat, not their story. The mikes are all wrong, and so is the subject: they prefer other stuff, more...acceptable stuff. James Roosevelt III for instance. He's here, looking rumpled as a good Democrat should. He'll speak shortly. We'll record him. That's nice and safe. He'll stand up there before the microphones and speak. Our audiences will love it.

"Yes," continues Gallagher, "at Warm Springs Roosevelt could be himself, and in his wheelchair or his little hand-controlled Ford he could go where he wished, when he wished.

"There was no pretense at Warm Springs; he was home. Here he was admired and loved and no one gave a damn whether or not he could walk."

Are they listening to that? The news director from CNN is smoking a cigarette, squatting, chatting with the cameraman. The producer from Channel 4 is looking at the ground.

"Elsewhere, in his public life Roosevelt was forced to perform a complex deception — emotional as well as physical — in order to deflect the public fears and hostility which all handicapped people must face.

"This performance was difficult and demanding; it greatly increased the burdens of the Presidency; and it certainly hastened his untimely death.

"Surely, today, forty years after his death, it is time to stop the pretense, drop the charade which society still expects of the handicapped...."

The speech is over. There is polite applause (overshadowed by someone over here under the large old oak, clapping a bit too loud and long, perhaps). Then cameras start to grind again. Roosevelt III gives his speech, and everyone is agog over whether he will be running for Tip O'Neill's seat, whether he'll make the announcement here in Georgia. After all — fifty years ago, important news used to be made here, important political news. Maybe we'll have something important happen here again, today. An announcement of candidacy — something important like that....

Dr. Waights G. Henry — Chancellor of LaGrange (Georgia) College — gives the keynote address. In his speech, Dr. Waights manages to get into everything (except the 1930 Ford Convertible resting nearby, safely behind glass): Herbert Hoover, the TVA, the NRA, the REA, the CCC, the ICU. The Supreme Court, the Wagner Act, the Four Freedoms, Yalta, Benito Mussolini ("upside down, strung up like a pig")[!]

"When I was graduating from Yale," says Dr. Waights G. Henry. "When I was in New Haven, graduating from Yale University," says Dr. Waights. "I saw Roosevelt only once, when I was graduating from Yale University. In New Haven, Connecticut. I was graduating from Yale, and Franklin Roosevelt was there, with his wife. He was there, to receive an honorary degree from Yale, at the same time of my graduation. From Yale University. In New Haven. When I was..."

Fortunately, the TV cameras were able to get the entire waight of his speech, as I watched a red bird over to the left, under a dogwood tree. Let me tell you. The Georgia cardinal wears a red that's so red it outdoes red. And the dogwood — so lovely in bloom, scarcely any leaves, the white flowers shower out by the hundreds, the tender white petals showering down by the thousands. The cardinal (red!) and the dogwood (white!) and I (me!) pay Dr. Waights no mind. We have other things to do. We have to pay attention to the sound, the special sound of the wind, coming so far from the east, coming to sing through the ten thousand pine needles overhead. We — bird, bush and I — listen to the way the branches catch the wind. We observe — the three of us — the movement of the whole tree. We appreciate that, and I don't believe we have time enough to pay much mind to Dr. Waights, and the way they stuck it to our good friend Hugh, in the way Roosevelt had been insulted hundreds of times. And — like FDR — never to say anything about it.

⧗

Speaking of insults, there was a final, special gift they laid — a black wreath — on our visit. Hugh and I and Paul (Paul is Hugh's able helpmeet) decided that we wanted to swim in the Warm Springs. 1200 gallons of eighty-six-degree water, pouring out of the ground. The very foundation of Warm Springs Foundation. That's why Roosevelt came here: he took the waters. He found that he could move in the warm waters, that they would help his muscles, his aching joints. Warm, laving, waters — the solid foundation of this institution.

We ask the Director of the Foundation, one E. Moran, to set it up so we can go swimming. That's how you do it now. You don't just go into the warm waters for a bracing, healthful swim. You go to the director, he fills out a requisition form, in triplicate, and that gets handed around, to the various other officials, and to the guard (they have guards now — just like in banks and prisons) and he, the guard, sets it up so you can take a swim.

The request gets lost somewhere. Me in my bathing trunks at eleven in the morning. "I don't see nothing here, Mr. Mylun," says the guard, guarding the waters. And I think: "They are spending $900,000 to refurbish the dining room. They have a staff of hundreds paid for by our generous taxes. They are embarking on a $62,000,000 fund-raising campaign so they can build some crazy sports rehab gymnasium complex over on the west campus. And I can't get a simple goddamn swim in the warm springs of Warm Springs." The wondrous magnetic waters bubbling out of the ground, there for the asking, except for my asking. They won't let me in the indoor pool, they close down the outdoor pool, fire the $2.35/hour lifeguard, board it up. They can't afford it, you know, what with the salaries and all…

⧗

"Roosevelt loved it because he could be himself here," said Gallagher in his speech. Me too. I loved it here because at one time, I could be myself here — swimming in the warm waters in the warm sunshine. But we have more pressing needs now, here at Georgia Warm Springs Foundation. We have to build buildings, raise money, put a public face in these buildings and grounds, hire some more guards...guards to guard the waters against all comers.

The old days...rehabilitation, gentleness, warmth, laughter, ease...openness to the visitors, the southern hospitality. That's all gone now, isn't it? Has to be. We have no room for it any more. We have so much fund-raising and building to do. You understand, don't you? There's just too much for us to do now.

IV. CRIPZEN

" *It was shocking to discover how confused and conditioned my mind was. Just sitting still, I found that I was not in control of my own thoughts or emotions — my mind had a mind of its own. It became clear to me that the untrained mind is a source of great delusion and suffering, both for myself and for others. I began to experience Buddhist meditation as an antidote to this condition, a comprehensive discipline that offers a different understanding of life, as well as another way of being in the world.*"

— *CRAZY WISDOM*
SCOOP NISKER

CRIPZEN

C RIPZEN BEGINS THE DAY YOU WAKE
up and know that you no longer own your body.
This takes longer than most of us realize, for there
is a part of the brain, the part responsible for our survival,
which repeats over and over again: "This has not happened
to me." Or, even more subtly, "This has happened to me,
but I've integrated it into my life, I've accepted it, I'm free."

During this period we survive by escaping.

Some escapes are standard, accepted in America,
and part of the operating system. Working. Getting drunk.
Sleeping. Taking tranquilizers. Watching TV. Brutalizing
wife, children, family, or friends. Getting God the Old
Testament Way.

There are other escapes that are a bit more far out,
and the folks that run the world will do something to us if
they find out that these are our preferences. Snorting or
shooting or selling illegal drugs. Stealing without specific
governmental permission. Attempted suicides. Going
mad.

Then there are escapes that in the long run turn out
not to be escapes at all but, rather, necessary steps on The
Path. These include getting involved in religions that
espouse more than hate or fear; or spending time with
teachers, prophets, or shrinks that have something grand to
teach us; or experimenting with drugs that open the door to
mystical experiences. And as part of these, the most important of them all — meditation.

In this book, I have counseled you to get free of the
prisons: those we build for ourselves, and those created by
people trying to help us. I have pointed out, for example,

that our families may love and revere us — but in the process, they can entrap us in their own special needs. I have suggested that in reaction to this, we may construct sympathetic traps that lead us to greater pain, if not self-destruction.

I have suggested that we can get free of both of these traps by experimentation, self-appraisal, and a powerful kindness to ourselves.

In experimentation, I have advised you to try new approaches to sex, some of which are fairly far out, but all of which share one vital characteristic: they take us *beyond* sex and on into tenderness and closeness to others (and yourself.) This means running roughshod over that part of the self that says, over and over again, "You're ugly. You don't deserve it. No one is ever going to love you because you're Crip." Those voices must be obviated.

For self-appraisal, I have recommended that you find a psychiatrist, psychologist, social worker or — best — a gathering of other Crips you can meet with, once a week or so, to deal with the truth of your body, and what it has done to your head. These meetings give you a chance to speak honestly with those who can hear you (often those closest to us have gone deaf because of *their* problems).

I will suggest, finally, that you open yourself up to what is going on within you. With certain experiments, you can begin to create a different view of your body and yourself. With this new perspective, you can actually begin to get rid of some of the poisons that plague us — regret, shame, depression, rage, denial, and self-pity — all cleverly hidden under a multitude of creative (and ruinous) disguises. By divesting yourself of the mock holiness that our culture assigns to our trauma, by recognizing the real pain that flows through us, and by listening to the gentle voice speaking inside, you can begin to enjoy a new way of dealing with yourself and the world that some may define as magic.[21]

⧗

We live in a country where the strange and the exotic are treated with contempt. Our careful Cartesian world casts these other-worldly experiences so far out to the edge that those of us who have the most to gain from experimenting with them are afraid to talk about them (much less try

---

[21]True mystical pursuits are not all that distant from the operative theories of psychiatry and psychology. All of them tell us to listen to the voice within. They teach us that underneath our self-destructive behavior patterns lives a entity that is wise, and that should be heeded. Shrinks call it "the subconscious," "the unconscious," or "the child within." The Quakers, the Hindus, and the Buddhists call it "the spirit," "Krishna," "the atman," or "the light." They're all talking about the same thing.

Readers may be confused by the fact that I urge both spiritual and psychological techniques for survival. I hasten to point out that the dichotomy most Americans assume between religion and psychiatry-psychology is often overstated. Carl Jung's fascination with Eastern religion was a key part of his writing and theory. (Indeed, he wrote the forward to the most popular edition of the *I Ching — The Book of Changes*). He also propounded the singular notion that all of humanity shares a "collective unconscious" that appears in many forms in our dreams and our fantasies. One of his own seminal experiences was an out-of-body experience when he was near death. He found himself lifted from his hospital bed to a nearby planet, where he entered a cave guarded by two angels. It was such an ecstatic experience that he wanted to stay and only returned, reluctantly, to continue his earthly life because he was told that he still had work to do here.

Freud is assumed to display even more distaste for the mystical-religious world. Yet he describes his warm friendship with the European poet and dramatist Romain Rolland, writer of several books on the lives of the mystics Ramakrishna and Vivekananda. Freud speaks of Rolland as one of the "few men from whom their contemporaries do not withhold admiration...one of these exceptional few [who] calls themselves my friend."

Freud tells us that Rolland spoke of a certain "sensation of 'eternity,' a feeling as of something limitless, unbounded — as it were, 'oceanic.'" He then states that he could not discover this "oceanic" feeling in himself, but then explains that it is "not easy to deal scientifically with feelings."

The surprise is not that Freud has trouble with "unscientific" feelings — he perceived that to be his job — but, rather, that he claims friendship, and a very warm friendship at that, with one of the greatest of European mystics, even to the point of giving an extended exegesis on what he called "falling out of the world." (See Part I of *Civilization and Its Discontents*.)

them) because we are afraid of being laughed at. Our Christian theologians who should be the avid proponents of magic (that's where they all came from) spit in the soup by considering any mystical experiences to be tainted. "The work of the devil," is the curse they lay on any divine inspiration outside of the straight, narrow, Biblical one. In this, they close many of us off from the rich experiences possible in our manifold journeys towards divinity.

For those of us who have lost some part of the physical self, spiritual experiences may well hold the key to part of our survival. Even more, they can permanently recast our view of death. Those who have embarked on these journeys uniformly report that their view of dying is profoundly changed from one of fear or indifference to one of acceptance.

We must allow ourselves to be free. This gives us the freedom to be less scornful of others who aren't, to be respectful of those who are more so, and — most of all — to be accepting of the spirit that grows within all of us, bidden or not.

If you are like me, you have times of desperation, times when you wake up at three A. M. and wonder what it all means, whether it's worth the candle. The Zen Buddhists say that these are the times when we are beginning on the Path.

Buddhists tell us that the body's pain, the body's pleasure — as well as book-learning, passion, hope, and hopelessness — may be illusional. You and I might be in an especially good position to study this.

Buddhists tell us that there is a paradox in pursuing exotic lust or exotic possessions or exotic foods for and with a body that soon enough must die. You and I are be in an especially good position to understand this.

Buddhists tell us that our need to travel, get rich, be entertained, or find love is far less important than seeking the peace within. You and I might be in an especially good position to experiment with this.

Buddhists ask us to pay special attention to birds, birdsong, trees, flowers, mountains and meadows — even a single stone in a single, small garden. You and I might be in an especially good position to try this.

Buddhists suggest that we can discipline our habits, our diets, and our thoughts, and that in doing so, we can leave a great deal of pain behind. You and I may be in an especially good position to begin this process.

Buddhists say that a divinity lies inside each of us, and the way to this divinity comes from stilling "the Monkey Mind;" this can be done, they say, through daily, serious meditation. You and I might be in an especially good position to experiment with this.

Buddhists tell us that once we start on the journey, we'll learn that ecstasy and agony are not too dissimilar, that happiness and sadness have the same roots, that our emotional ups are neither more important nor more to be desired than our emotional downs. Exhilaration and depression, joy and sorrow, "good" mood and "bad" moods need not be pitted against each other, for they come out of the same place: our heads.

They even have a word for these ups and downs. They're called "illusions."

◻

When one ignorant attains realization he is a saint.
When a saint begins to understand he is ignorant.
It is better to realize mind than body.
When mind is realized one need not worry about body.
When mind and body become one
The man is free...[22]

Once you begin to go through the literature of Buddhism, Zen Buddhism, Hinduism, Yoga, and Taoism, you'll find that they all direct you to a simple, basic, one-step Way. Meditation.

Meditation. Stilling the noisy mind. In a quiet environment, once or twice a day, making the mind shut up for ten or fifteen minutes, so that you can gradually have revealed to you the diamond within. You are it.

You must stand warned, however, that those who try out these "exotic" religions often reach a point — after reading and studying and experimenting — where they start singing the old Peggy Lee song "Is That All There Is?" It's so simple, and at times so slow, that they think (the busy-bee mind again), "I'm not getting anything out of this stuff. Big deal."

Actually it is a Big Deal.

Because meditation isn't what you think.

◻

Instead of repeating here the writings of thousands of teachers on Buddhism, Hinduism, and meditation, I

---

[22]*Zen Flesh, Zen Bones*, compiled by Pau Reps. Anchor Books, 1989.

have included in the next few chapters specific steps for quieting the mind. These chapters, written in collaboration with the noted neo-mystic Carlos Amantea, will give you techniques for how-to-do-it, plus offering extensive quotes from several of the best writers on the subjects.

In addition, I list below several books to teach you further techniques for meditation and religious study. Included are self-hypnosis, dream, out-of-body work and other suggestions for getting on The Path.

Of all the books listed, *We're All Doing Time* is probably the best distillation of the manifold techniques of meditative peace and vision (for the world; for the self.) It was written for prisoners and put together by one of the true sages that pop up from time to time like a balloon in our culture — Bo Lozoff. (Hi, Bo. Are you still meditating fifteen hours a day? Stop it. Your fans need you.)

The other books will give you background for new experiments with your mind. These may be the last (and best) journeys that we will be allowed to take, ones that will profoundly alter your view of the divine from within and from without.

Some of these journeys will be very strange, and you will find their inclusion here equally strange. For example, one of the suggestions is that you consider experimenting with psychedelic drugs, even though such fooling around is considered slightly below child molestation as the super No-No of our times. The American Judicial system murders people (or puts them in jail, which is the same thing) for buying, selling, or using LSD or other psychedelics. And yet, for many, a careful, well-planned trip on acid or

peyote may well open that tiny door hidden in the wall — a
door to you that you would never find any other way.[23]

---

[23]It is important to separate the Learning Drugs from the the Unlearning Drugs. The
former, include LSD, peyote, San Pedro, hashish, marijuana, magic mushrooms,
MDMA and DMT. The Unlearning Drugs (so-called because they brutalize rather
than enhance one's vision) are cocaine, crack, meth, PCP, crystal, all tranquilizers,
and "free-base," among others. The pain-killers (codeine, heroin, methadone,
darvon, and daludid) are in a different category entirely, and we can make no
judgment on the use of them by those who may need to do so.

We must strongly caution those who want to experiment with the Learning
Drugs that there are five rules for a safe and sane trip:

1) Realize that these drugs are immensely powerful. Indeed, LSD is so powerful
that it creates attacks of paranoic schizophrenia in those who just *think about it*. The
gravest of these "contact-high" schizophrenics live at the DEA and within the
chambers of the United States Supreme Court. They have determined that if you are
caught with LSD, your time in jail will depend on the weight of the container, as
well as the amount of the drug itself. This can mean that being caught with a tiny
amount of the drug can result in up to twenty years a federal pen — the worst trip
of them all. Act accordingly — which means,

2) Know your sources.

3) Don't go on a journey on psychedelics alone or with people who are
unexperienced. Find someone who has been there before, so he or she can guide you
over the shoals.

4) Make your journey in a peaceful setting — away from all distractions,
noises, crowds (and the Supreme Court) (and the DEA).

5) Read up before you make the journey. The books listed here (especially
those of Leary, Ram Dass, Watts and Stafford) are a must.

SELECTED READINGS

We're All Doing Time by Bo Lozoff. Written in non-technical language for prisoners, filled with techniques on meditation, survival, and forgiving an unforgiving world. You and I (indeed all of us) are in prison, and the way out is described in easy-to-comprehend, artlessly artful language. You would be well off to order his other spiritual book as well, *Just Another Spiritual Book*. (Send $25 for both to Prison Ashram Project, Rt 1, Box 201-N, Durham NC 27705)

Journeys Out of the Body by Robert Monroe is the classic on OOB experiences. Simple, direct, filled with anecdotes and a how-to-do-it. (Doubleday/Anchor)

When The Swans Came To The Lake by Rick Fields is an impartial and lively description of the roots of Buddhism in America, starting with the Transcendentalists, complete with descriptions of some of the masters still practicing. (Snow Lion)

Memories, Dreams, Reflections by Carl Jung. Jung's autobiography is a tale of a fascinating life — he was one of the originators of the concept of psychotherapy — but describes several of his mystical and OOB experiences as well. (Vintage)

The Sound of the One Hand, by Yoel Hoffman. An excellent introduction to the paradoxical questions-and-answers of Zen Buddhism. Includes 281 Zen koans, with extended discourses on the possible answers. (Bantam).

Zen Flesh, Zen Bones, by Paul Reps. Selections of early Zen writings. (Anchor/Doubleday)

Aghora: *At the Left Hand of God* by Robert E. Svoboda. Aghora was able to teletransport himself to exotic Parisian restaurants, and spent some of his happiest hours at the ghats (the places where bodies are burned) alongside the Ganges. He and his eccentric, often riotous philosophy, are described in detail by one of his followers. Some have called him the Charles Bukowski of mysticism. (Brotherhood of Life, 110 Dartmouth SE, Albuquerque NM 871061)

The Complete Works of Swami Vivekananda. Eight-volume set describing the New Hinduism started a century ago by Ramakrishna. Vivekananda was one of his most articulate followers, and in his speeches and writings, describes in vivid detail the philosophy and practice of the fourth largest religion in the world. (Advaita Ashrama: available at Vedanta Societies in major cities in the United States.)

Tibetan Yoga and Secret Doctrines, edited by W. Y. Evans-Wentz. Far more meaningful than the more famous *Tibetan Book of the Dead*, *Tibetan Yoga* describes specific meditations out of what some call the purest branch of Buddhism. (Oxford University Press)

How To Know God by Swami Prabhavananda and Christopher Isherwood. One of the landmark books on yoga: the Sutras of Patanjali translated into simple, easy, direct English — with extended commentaries. (Mentor)

The Mahabarata. A superb translation of the epic poem of India by Jean-Claude Carriére. The original is ten times longer than the Bible — but here it is condensed down to a six-hour stage play. (Perennial/Harper & Row)

Yoga for the Disabled by Howard Kent. Once you get over his rather judgmental view of what has happened to us, there are some very important exercises, along with advice on posture and attitude. (Thorsons Publishing)

Crazy Wisdom, by Wes "Scoop" Nisker. An overview of the universe, drugs, Zen, saints, philosophers, poets, fools, and what-it-all-means. Includes some of the best definitions extant of the differences between the Western religions and the Eastern. (Ten-Speed Press)

The Spirit of Zen, by Alan Watts. Watts was one of the most important translators of what he called Philosophy East for the West. The writings are witty, the words down-to-earth, and the insights profound. (Pantheon)

Be Here Now by Ram Dass. The earliest and most popular — and some would say the best — introduction to some of the fallacies of Western religions and the power of Eastern ones. (Lama Foundation)

The Psychedelic Experience by Tim Leary and Ram Dass. An explication of the world of LSD and peyote by two of the earliest exponents. Definitely a book of the 60s.

The Psychedelic Encyclopaedia, by Peter Stafford. A complete, thoughtful, and up-to-date disquisition on the history, use, and availability of various psychedelic drugs — including a listing of some that are still legal. Third revised edition. (Ronin Press)

Ecstasy — the MDMA Experience, by Bruce Eisner. Some call it the gentlest of the psychedelics. Eisner describes its uses and cautions against its abuse. (Ronin Press)

Fighting Through Spiritual Materialism, by Choygam Trungpa. Even though this master is now discredited — he was a boozer and a womanizer who went around in the buff (with a red ribbon tied around his cock) — this is one of the honest and true books about the road to spiritualism. (Shambala)

Seeds of Wisdom: A Garland of Modern Meditations, by Elizabeth Gips. A survivor of the Haight-Ashbury shares her learned experiences of meditation for survival. (Self-published and available from Audiodelics, Box 7305, Santa Cruz CA 95060. $15 plus $2 postage.)

The Sun: A Magazine of Ideas, edited by Sy Safransky. Essential monthly reading for those interested in the soul and freedom (and freedom of the soul) without all the hackneyed verbiage of the so-called "New Age" magazines. ($30 a year from *The Sun*, 107 N. Roberson, Chapel Hill, NC 27516)

V. FOUR PATHS

Master Hōen said, "It is like a cow passing throught a window frame. The head, the horns, the four legs have all gone through; why can't the tail go through?"

— *THE SOUND OF THE ONE HAND*
YOEL HOFFMAN

INTRODUCTION
By Carlos Amantea

THERE ARE SEVERAL WAYS OF KEEPING the mind quiet, stopping it from being so noisy and tangling up our lives. You can also use these methods to untangle parts of yourself.

The four techniques we have found to be most useful are direct meditation, self-hypnosis, astra-projection, and dream-work. These will be described in succeeding chapters.

Remember that these techniques for spiritual growth should be accompanied by a conscious revision of your living habits. You should change what goes into your body, and — at the same time — what runs through (and runs) your mind.

Your diet should include only the healthiest foods — salads, vegetables, beans, pure rice, fish and shellfish, and soy proteins. You should begin to limit your consumption of rich dairy products, meats, and salt and sugar. You should also limit your intake of most drugs, alcohol, and colas.

You should strive to downplay anger and the angry thoughts you may have towards the world, your family, and the people around you. Anger can here be defined as any form of rage you may aim at others, as well as any cruelty that you may direct towards youself. (Discovering that these exist in you — and run your relationships with the world — is half the battle).

As you progress along the path, you'll find that vindictiveness will become rare; forgiveness should become your staple. When you find yourself falling into anger or

self-pity (they both come out of the same roots) it will help
to avail yourself of one of the meditative devices described
in the following chapters.

Most of all, you should begin the work of self-
integration — the deep and necessary process of accepting
where you are, forgiving who you are, and recalling how
you got there. If you concentrate once or twice a day on the
nugget of saintliness that rests inside all of us, you can begin
this process of self-realization, acceptance and forgiveness.
In this way, Norman Vincent Peale (who we have often
mocked) has one gem of truth: if you feel crappy about
yourself, you will feel crappy about the whole world, and
your place in it.

It should be your job through meditation, self-
hypnosis, or a simple daily mantra to give abundant caring
to yourself. It may offend you to read the self-serving
bumper-stickers ("Damn I'm Good"), but you can devise
one for yourself that is honest and serves to reaffirm your
faith in you. Hang it on the wall or on the mirror (or, if you
must, on the bumper of your car). Have it there so you can
tell yourself, regularly, that you are not a jerk.

A friend of mine got stuck with the word "stupid."
Throughout her youth, that was what her brothers and
sisters called her when she did something they didn't like.
She internalized it and laid it on herself everytime she did
something bad or wrong. After becoming paraplegic, she
thought it everytime she did something awkward like spill-
ing something, making an inelegant move, or falling down.

After some soul-searching, she figured that the
word "stupid" was not appropriate nor servicable any
longer, especially for some small and unavoidable error. She
reasoned that she was hurting herself three times: once by

her accident, second by a simple slip, and finally by buying into a word they had laid on her so many years ago. She decided that she should discard it for something better; that instead, when she fell, she could say something useful like, "I'm sorry, did you hurt yourself?" She even began to apply an affectionate word to herself, a word usually reserved for a family member, or a lover. It may sound sappy and sentimental, but she found this simple present to herself was a gift that worked to keep her from damaging herself further.

⧗

As we have indicated, your new path should always start with a daily meditation.

For those who have lived and studied other religions, there are two potent images of meditation — one from the nineteenth century, one from the twentieth.

The first comes from Yogananda's *Autobiography of a Yoga*, the classical work on eastern religion in the western world. Yogananda describes an evening when he and his master were together for the evening's meditation. They were in a damp field, at nightfall. Yogananda reports: "He sat down in the lotus position on the wet ground, and fell immediately in a trance. It was not so easy for me, because during the whole time, the mosquitoes were like a grey, heavy blanket all over us — over face, hands, feet, and body. The strength of his meditation was such that he didn't even notice them."

The second comes from a photograph taken in 1967, in front of the American Embassy in Viet Nam. To protest the war, a Buddhist monk sat down in the lotus position, poured gasoline over his body, and lit a match. As he was being consumed by the flames, he was not thrashing about, nor screaming, as you and I might have done. Far from it: he died still seated in the lotus position, moveless, meditating deeply as the flames were enveloping his body, his face, and his hair. He never moved as the flames rendered him bone and ash.

Thus the power of meditation.

⧗

All around us, noisy men with a disbelief in the simple goodness of life contend among themselves. They fill themselves with a tiny, proctological view of the world; they proclaim an angry god who rains down fire and destroys with sickness and accidents those who disagree with them.

For those of us who sense a more gentle universe, there are other divines available who offer more than fire, brimstone, and terror. These are the quieter gods who suffuse the universe with subtle colors and musics, vibrate in a throbbing song of harmony, and can erupt in soaring multi-colored flames, a rainbow light-in-dark that reveals to us the beginnings of the incomprehensible.

They may call to us in Hindi or Tibetan or Mandarin Chinese. They may speak silently through and with a roomful of people who say nothing, but remain peacefully in divine spirit. They may dance in the dust of the village as an old Black man on a cane, bringing visions through his serpent of visions. They may cry out in a deep valleys, echoing calls and songs that ring the shadows, pulse with what some might confuse with passion.

They may frieze in the stars of the night. They may rise up out of a dark meadow to confront us with our sadness. They may blast out of billowing volcanoes, or may follow the simple path of the yellow-black butterfly across the garden.

They may, as one of my friends has it, merely (merely!) turn up in the mu-mesons that pour through our universe in such dark, ineluctable, unmeasurable, undetectible profusion (a billion of them have just passed through your body and are well on their way to Pluto in the time it takes you to read this sentence), beings who will return to us — to shape us and change us — when we are ready.

A choosing of the gods is a fine task, and a blessing. It is one that gives us the freedom to move beyond those who use the divine to condemn, rather than love. We can thus choose an ecstatic god to guide us into a kindness to ourselves, and a new kindness to others.

The Twelve Step people may be right: we don't need to be specific about The Who It Is we choose to be our god or gods. All we have to do is to acknowledge that there is another power about, one that is more kindly and heroic than the vengeful god that most humans choose to devise for themselves, and for others. We can, like them, seek our gods in and through the mirror; but, unlike them, we can seek what we see with affection, rather than anger.

1. MEDITATION

MASTER: *This cow — when was it born?*
STUDENT: *It was born before this world began.*
MASTER: *Is it a female cow? A male cow?*
STUDENT: *It's a huge-balls-hanging-down male cow.*
MASTER: *What's its color?*
STUDENT: *The cloak is iron-blue, the kimono is gray, the underwear is white....*

— *THE SOUND OF THE ONE HAND*

MEDITATION IS HARD FOR EVERYBODY, *because we've all allowed our minds to run wild for many years. It takes time and effort to regain our rightful control, but it's well worth the discipline. An uncontrolled mind — no matter how much it knows, how smart it becomes, or how many pleasures it experiences — will never find peace or satisfaction. As soon as we fulfill one part of it, it'll hit us with another demand, another question, another passing thought... The mind can be a great servant, but a cruel and exhausting master.*[24]

To begin, most teachers suggest that you find a quiet place to sit comfortably — or however comfortably those of us without functioning arms or legs can be expected to do so. If you can, find a place where you will not be disturbed for half-an-hour or so.

Begin by breathing in and out deeply two or three times, and then, with a normal respiration, keep the eyes focused gently on some object a few feet before you (candle-flame, intaglio, spot-in-the-wall.) Or you can focus on

---

[24]*We're All Doing Time*, Page 29.

the very act of breathing, putting your concentration on the place where air enters your nose. This is Lozoff's method:

> *One of the most universal meditation methods is to use your own breath as the one-point of concentration. After getting the body silent, bring all your attention to one of these two points: the tip of your nose, where the breath automatically goes in and out, or the lower abdomen, where the diaphragm rises with each in-breath, and falls with each out-breath.*
>
> *Whether you choose the nose or the diaphragm, keep the mind right there, feeling the whole movement of each breath in and out. Don't follow it in or out; just keep the attention in one spot, observing however it feels as it goes by.*
>
> *The breath is a very good one-point for concentration, because it's fresh every second; it helps us bring the mind into the present moment. And the present moment is the only place that true meditation ever happens (in fact, it's the only place anything ever really happens).*
>
> *Time and time again — maybe hundreds of times in a half-hour — the mind will wander, and you'll forget all about observing your breath. But the instant you remember that you forgot, simply drop the chain of thoughts in mid-stream, and get right back to the nose or the diaphragm…*
>
> *There's no sense being frustrated by distractions, because the frustration is just another distraction. Remember, this isn't really meditation, anyway; it's meditation practice. If we were already good at it, we wouldn't need to practice.*

When using the breath as a meditation method, it's not necessary to breathe any special way, or to try to control the breathing at all. The idea is to observe the breath however it is.[25]

You should spend fifteen or twenty minutes sitting thus — once shortly after getting up in the morning, then again in the late afternoon or early evening.

You should do it at the same time and same place each day, and should be sure that you are not interrupted by telephones or people or food-trays. If your thoughts keep intruding, send them quietly and gently packing — and return to the quiet meditative state.

When you are done, you should bring yourself back to the world as gently as possible, taking in a deep breath, and acknowledging the "coming down" state with thanks.

Some masters tell us that we can only do meditation in the lotus position. Obviously, they haven't gone through Rehab. Meditation can be done in the normal sitting position, but many of us are not able to get into the sitting position without falling on our faces.[26] No mind — as you are lying flat on your back, or in a slightly raised bed, or even lying on your side, you can give yourself fifteen or thirty minutes of peace each day. Ask those around you to be quiet for awhile, and have the curtains drawn. Choose a special place in the ceiling, and, breathing slowly and regularly, watch it. Any thoughts that flit into the brain

[25]*We're All Doing Time*, Page 33.

[26]Elizabeth Gips, in *Seeds of Wisdom*, states that the lotus position may not be necessary at all: *Traditional meditation tells us that the spine must be straight to allow energy to rise up it, and that if we lock in our own energy by making outselves into a sort of physical pretzel, it will be easier to get into a true meditative state. With all due respect, that is not my experience. Try different postures and see which ones work best for you.*

should be set aside gently so that you can concentrate on the nothing that is everything. When you prepare to reenter the world, do it without haste. Blink your eyes, breathe deeply and thank that part of your mind that made it possible for you to have this few minutes of peace.

If you live in a place where such silence and privacy is totally impossible, set up a time for yourself before dawn where there is the best chance of quiet. Program yourself to wake at that time. Get yourself into a comfortable position and concentrate, and breathe. Don't fall asleep: the right degree of concentration is necessary to keep from doing this. (Once I had the nurses hang a small luminous disc on an overhead bar where I could look at it at certain times of the night. It usually worked to keep me awake.)

As you start this discipline, it is valuable to keep a perspective on it. There won't be any fireworks, at least not at first. There will be times when you are wondering what the hell you are doing, and why. Just set these doubts aside, and go ahead with it. Remember — Buddhists and Hindus have been meditating thus for thousands of years, and many have achieved insight into themselves and the universe by what seems to be a deceptively simple procedure.

At first you will find it difficult to keep thoughts from cluttering up your brain. But remember that all this interior chatter (what they call "The Monkey Mind") merely clouds the clear lake of our true self. Once we begin to discipline the mind, the turbidity settles out, and the Real You begins to rise out of the obscurity. As you work through this, you will find sooner or later that your thoughts will choose on their own to keep out of the way. As one master said — this is when we come to own our own thoughts. With this control a power comes that lets us begin to create a peace, a peace that makes it possible to survive in even the most impossible of worlds.

One interesting variation of this is a Yogic Meditation that was used with quadriplegics in one of the Los Angeles hospitals. They were told to clear their minds, and as they went into the relaxed state, they began exercises with their "aetheric" bodies. (The theory is that inside the "real" body is a more nebulous electrical force that constitutes the "aetheric" body. This is what moves out of us during out-of-body experiences.)

Participants were told to move their "aetheric" arms out to the front, then to the back, then to the front, then back, then down. In another exercise, they were told to stretch their "aetheric" arms and legs as far out as possible — and hold them there.

A more down-to-earth form of exercise is offered by Howard Kent in *Yoga for the Disabled*:

Keeping the shoulders still, breathe in and then, breathing out, slowly turn the head to the right. When the breath stops, stop the movement. Breathe in again without moving the head, allowing it to move further round again on the out-breath. The same thing can be done a third time until the head is turned to the greatest possible degree without pressure. Then, breathing in, the head is slowly turned to the front and, breathing out, to the left. The same process is adopted of moving the head only on the out-breath. Once again, breathing in, bring the head to the front, and breathing out, let the chin drop on the chest. Now let each out-breath make the head feel heavier, so the back of the neck is stretched. After several breaths, bring the head up, breathing in and let it loll against the back of the neck.

Clench the jaw and let it fall more heavily back with each out-breath, finally bring the head to an upright position once more. This form of head movement, using relaxation of the out-breath at all times, is excellent for removing the tension suffered by those in wheelchairs.[27]

---

[27]Scoop Nisker in *Crazy Wisdom* offers several other possible forms of meditation:
In most types of meditation, one must first break through the rational, analytic mode of understanding. One way of doing this is to throw the rational mind an impossible question called a koan...a riddle meant to short-circuit all logical connections. The method, referred to as "using poison against poison," frustrates the thinking mind until it breaks down. The answer to any koan lies in letting go of the desire to understand it logically. On some level, the answer to any koan riddle is "I don't know." The koan teaches what Alan Watts called "the wisdom of insecurity" — how to live with doubt and even embrace it. With the koan we learn to have questions without needing answers.

Zen practice is said to have 1,700 koans. Three of the most famous are: "What is the sound of one hand clapping?" "If everything returns to the One, to what does the One return?" "Does a dog have Buddha nature?..."

Other techniques for beginning meditation include the mantra (repetition of phrases or patterns of syllables), visualization (holding images steady in the mind), and concentration on a single object or action, such as one's breath. These practices develop strength and focus of mind, enabling meditators to see through their individual obsessions and confusion to discover what is often referred to as our "true nature..."

Meditation is commonly called a "practice," because meditators practice living in this mind — the mind of "clarity." They practice an ongoing watchfulness of their mental and emotional life. This practice should not be confused with Western psychology, which studies the individual's personal story. In meditation, one learns to go beyond personality and becomes aware of the mechanics of the mind and emotions. Meditation can teach the physics of the psyche — the origin of thoughts and feelings, and how they interact. It can help to free us from our instincts as well as our ideologies. Meditation cultivates equanimity and peace in the mind; it frees us from the psyche's drama, allowing us to just be present in each moment.

2. SELF-HYPNOSIS

MASTER: *How does it feed?*

STUDENT: *For breakfast, wheat porridge; for lunch, the regular meal; for dinner, rice and vegetable porridge.*

MASTER: *Where is the cow?*

STUDENT: *"I sit by myself in the deep and quiet bamboo forest,
Playing music and howling out long."*

MASTER: *Where is its birthplace?*

STUDENT: *An octagonal millstone spinning in midair.*

— THE SOUND OF THE ONE HAND

SELF-HYPNOSIS MAY BE JUST ANOTHER branch of meditation. For some of us it is far simpler because the busy-body mind is given a task that helps to calm it, a "count down."

Get in a comfortable position either sitting or lying in a quiet environment. Close the eyes, and say to yourself "Relax" as you count backwards on the outbreath. Thus, you will breathe in slowly, and then, as you exhale, you will say to yourself "Ten [pause] Relax." Next outbreath: "Nine [pause] Relax." "Eight [pause] Relax." Go slowly all the way to "Zero [pause] Relax." Then breathe in, go back to ten and start the count-down again. If you begin to drift off, it may be rewarding to tell yourself at some point, "When I awake, I will be relaxed and refreshed..."

It often helps to visualize the numbers as you are counting. You may go down in an elevator, passing large numbers pasted on the wall. Or you may move slowly down on a ramp or moving stairs, passing numbers that mark the journey down into a bucolic garden, filled with flowers and trees and peace.

How will you know when you are there? Trust me: you'll know. The world will seem a little more contained. Your "vision" will narrow down. Thoughts will not rise up to bother you, or — if they do — they will be more distant.

And when you allow yourself to awaken, your body will confirm that you have been in a trance. For me, it is a tell-tale numbness of thumb and forefinger of my left hand. When I go into deeper trances, I can actually measure the depth by the level of numbness up my left arm.

If you do this count-down at bedtime, or when you are tired — you will often put yourself in a trance and, at the same time, send yourself off into sleep.[28] Not to fear: when the time to awaken comes, you'll do so easily.

These techniques do not work well if you are on tranquilizers, pain or sleeping pills. If you are in a situation where you are forced to take medication, ask your "care-givers" if they can let you go twenty-four hours without such pills or shots. If they will not permit that, try to time your experiments with self-hypnosis as far away from pill-taking time as possible.

---

[28]I had taken sleeping pills for almost thirty years until I stumbled across self-hypnosis. Since then, I very rarely take sleeping pills, knowing, as I do, that they vitiate the dream process (see below.)

3. ASTRAL PROJECTION

MASTER: *Why can't the tail go through?*
STUDENT: [Holding the master by the nose, slapping the
master's rear] *Even if I say giddy-up, he doesn't
budge an inch.* [Sings]
*"Where is the person with whom we came together
to appreciate the moon?*
*The scenery looks very much the same as that of last
year."*
[The student gets on all fours and like a cow
crawls around the room].

— *THE SOUND OF THE ONE HAND*

ONE OF THE MOST UNUSUAL MEDITA-
tive experiences is called astral projection. With
this, one is allowed to fly out of the body, either
to visit known places, or to go to other lands and other
worlds. The best times for out-of-body experiences are
when one is between the sleep-wake state, either falling
asleep, or waking up.

If you ever wake up in the hypnogogic state (charac-
terised by an intense buzzing in the ears, a movelessness
and an hypertrophied sense of the body around the body),
you will easily be able to move the "aetheric" body about.
Even without it, you should attempt to catch yourself in
that frozen moment between sleep and awakening where
you can begin the process of escape.

You begin by rotating the body about the spine.
This is done by *thinking* yourself in motion. If you are
successful, the aetheric body will begin to move "like a pig

revolving on a spit above the fire" (the words of one practicioner.)

You will find as this other body disentangles from the real (or everyday) body, you can propel yourself out of the room, going through walls or floors with little or no effort. Some people hold objects in their hands like fans or toy propellers to pull or push them out and into space. One student told of moving her feet like rotors to propel herself (this from a person who in "real life" could not move anything from the chest down.)

You will know that your aetheric body is being separated from your "other" body because it will feel like it is being *bathed in diamonds* (as it has been described.) If you lose your concentration, or begin to think you are making a fool of youself, you will lose the power and the movement and fall back into yourself. However, if you continue to push gently out of yourself, through the wall, into the outer world, you will be on a glorious journey into hyperspace.

Can you get stuck out there? It's rare but possible, wrote Monroe in the classic *Journeys Out of the Body*. In a famous quote, he describes trying to return to his sleeping body and running slam-bang into a stone wall. No matter how he tried, he could not pass through that wall: there seemed to be no top, no bottom, no end of it.

After a moment of panic, he did what any good astral projector would do: he took a contrary route. He turned around and flew in the opposite direction, the direction he had earlier thought would be *away* from his sleeping self. Within a trice, he was back in his own body again.

This teaches us, once again, that the way to survive — in the world or out of it — is not by resisting ("kicking against the pricks," in the Biblical phrase), but to go with the flow, even if it threatens to take us in the "wrong" direction.

"When I used to wake up in the hypnogogic state," wrote one observer, "I was panic-stricken. I'd fight against it, trying desperately to move a finger or open my eyes. After reading Monroe's book, however, when I wake in that state, rather than fight it, I immediately start rotating my body about the spine to free it, so I can take off and begin to fly. No effort is needed except to restrain my crazy enthusiasm for getting the hell out of my body. However, when I get excited I often awaken at once, and have to resume my hum-drum life in the 'real' world, in my 'real' body again — missing yet another exciting journey."

4. DREAM WORK

MASTER: *What's the form of the cow?*
[The student moves forward and backward, left, and right].
MASTER: *What's the height of the cow?*
[The student gives his own height].
MASTER: *Is it a male cow? A female cow?*
[The student sticks his nose in front of the master, and says, "Moo."]

— *THE SOUND OF THE ONE HAND*

YOUR DREAMS HAVE MANY MESSAGES for you, and by working with them, you can learn a great deal about yourself.

Dreams are symbols — pictures, images, code — being transmitted from one portion of your brain to another.[29] These symbols constitute a communication that goes on all hours of the day and night inside your head whether you choose to tune in or not. This television set within you is probably more important than the other one, the one you watch all day, every day. The commercials are a bit different, the messages a bit more noble.

To begin dream work, you must have a pen and a pad near at hand to write down the dream the moment you wake up. If you don't do this, your dream work will be meaningless because dreams evaporate as quickly as the

---

[29]Some would call these parts of the brain "primitive." Perhaps it is better to think of them as the child that lies within all of us, a child that does not communicate with written or spoken words, only with images.

Of all the 20th century artists, Laurie Anderson has discovered how best to communicate with this child-in-the-psyche. It is worth your while to rent or borrow the video called *Home of the Brave*. It will show you how she communicates with this preverbal part of us.

dew. The pad and pen on your bedtable become a mnemonic device to urge you to remember to write down what you have just seen and heard.

Write without comment, using detail and simple words. Instead of saying "A horrible monster threatened me," write "A large tiger with a rose in one ear came up out of the sewer and I thought he was going to eat me but he kissed me instead." Instead of "I saw a woman and she was very beautiful and I loved her" write "She had large grey eyes, a gentle mouth, and as she moved closer and closer to me, I realized she reminded me of the goddess of love." If the dream is very long and complex, you should write down key words to help jog your memory for writing later on, for these details can disappear quickly into the mist.

Sometime later the same day, you should divide the page in half and rewrite your dream as fully as possible on the left-hand side of the page. On the right, you should jot down feelings: those you had when you were dreaming, or those that erupt as you are writing down the dream. You should also put down ideas about what each of the symbols may mean to you.

Let's say you dream about a great golden elephant kneeling on the high mountain, and the wind comes up and blows him to earth where he is revealed as nothing more than a thin piece of gold-foil.

You would want to ask yourself — and write down — answers to the following questions:

Why an elephant? (What does an elephant mean to you — not to the world, but to you? What has been your experience with elephants? What do you feel about them: fear? joy? hate? love? interest?)

Why kneeling? (What does kneeling mean to you?
What does a kneeling elephant mean to you?)

Why is there gold-leaf? (What has been your experience with gold, and with leaves?)

What does it mean to you that a huge kneeling elephant drifts gently to the ground and disappears into a little heap of foil?

Remember to note all puns. Even the silliest can convey important messages.[30]

There are no dream books that can tell you what these pictures mean. The dream is yours, you are it. As you review it and meditate on it, you should dip into your beliefs, your history, and most of all your feelings to find the story the dream-machine is telling you.

Dreams are very specific, and they address specific events that have gone on or are going on in your heart and soul and life and loves. No-one holds the key but you. No matter how weird the dream, you should write it down in its entirety and preserve it and give it the chance to tell you something about yourself.[31]

I keep my dreams in a separate notebook, and often will go back and review them a month or a year later to see

---

[30]I once dreamed repeatedly of ears of corn. I finally figured out it was reference to my dubious talent of hearing words and making them "corny," that is, being able to pun with them.

[31]Sometimes dreams tend to be more cosmic. Recently, I dreamed that I understood the why of AIDS. In my dream, I saw it as the disease of the 21st Century. AIDS exists because in the last fifty years we have create a multitude of medicines to "cure" every conceivable sickness. But we aren't and never have *cured* disease. What we are doing is redesigning infirmities and our own RNA so that we can be temporarily free of the natural flow and purge that is sickness.

This is buying from the future, and thus is only a temporary solution. Illnesses is a cure (that is what inoculation is all about; some would say that death is the ultimate cure.) By not permitting this natural purge of diseases, we open the door for opportunistic infections to mutate so that they can revisit us in more virulent forms. We have merely redesigned ourselves and our illnesses so that when they come to us, they do so in a ruinous fashion.

if I can dig up any nuggets that I lost the first or second time around. I have even gone back to dreams that I wrote down years ago. I am always amazed at the power they still have over me. I often find myself tense or excited when reviewing them, as tense or excited as I was when I had the dream itself.

I often find myself smiling too, at the clear truths the dreams were telling me from so long ago. One dream from 1956 was of my shrink as a fussy old lady, sitting in a rocking chair. As I look back on my experience with Dr. Clark — a male Jungian MD who first had me write down my dreams — I realize that although I didn't think it much at the time, he *was* a bit fussy, and slightly feminine. (I often wonder what he thought about as I read him this dream.)

As you work with dreams, you will find symbols that recur again and again. They can be persons, objects, feelings. Dogs, ducks, rocks, trees, places where you have been (or have never been) and specific people (old lost friends, presidents, the guy at the corner deli who you think certainly doesn't belong in your dreams — but he does: that's why he's there). I often dream of the "sophisticated lady," a no-nonsense woman who stands up in my dreams to explain what is happening. Before, I puzzled over her until I realized I was being shown what Jung called the "anima," the feminine part of me: sharp, wise, no nonsense, instinctive. When I was growing up, this aspect of myself was held to be "sissy," but I realize now that she was and is a very special, artful part of myself. "I came to see that this inner feminine figure plays a typical, or archetypal, role in the unconscious of a man, and I called her the 'anima,'" said Carl Jung in *Memories, Dreams and Reflections*. (The corresponding figure in the unconscious of woman he called the "animus.")

Some dream workers are able — with experience — to enter their dreams and affect the outcome of the action. The Senoi, inhabitants of a Pacific island, spend their mornings telling each other their dreams and commenting on them. Researchers have reported that they teach themselves how to intervene in the dreams. It is Senoi dream tradition that when they are being chased by some animal, they turn on the pursuer, and demand a gift. (It is said that the animal always complies. It is also said that the Senoi are some of the world's gentlest people.)

When you try self-hypnosis, you can ask the Dream Machine for a specific dream. I once experimented: in the hypnotic state, I asked for a good old-fashioned lust-passion (ideally: wet) dream. It happened that very night: I dreamed about having sex. It was a Lust Bomb: we indulged ourselves in an astonishing number of positions in our fore- and after-play. Unfortunately, it was with a rather dominating lady I had known years before, that I certainly no longer cared for (or even wanted to remember.)

At times, you will have a genuine Aha! experience as you go through your dreams. Symbols that recur will begin to have meaning for you. This gives you the chance to recast your views about yourself and your past. The things that seemed so dreadful to you when you were a child will come to be less dreadful; things you had seen as inconsequential will come to be more important. For years, I persuaded myself that the ten days I was in high fever in the hospital in 1952 were of little importance — that only the change in my body held the key to what I later felt (and feared). But constant dreams about gentle grey birds trapped in a cage during a fire finally told me that the time of fever had affected me — my mind, my soul, my boyhood. My brain was that gentle bird in the cage, and the fire the fever had scarred it viciously. Having grown up in a house and culture where madness was much derided and greatly feared, I experienced going crazy — the bird the mind trying to escape from that room of fire — as a trauma that took thirty long, hard, painful years to forgive.

My dreams and I are still working on it.

APPENDICES

" *Though I am now disillusioned, I cannot think about the cooling of the sun without fear. I don't mind if my fellow men forget about me the day after I'm buried. As long as they're alive, I'll haunt them, unnamed, imperceptible, present in every one of them just as the billions of dead who are unknown to me and whom I preserve from annihilation are present in me. But if mankind disappears, it will kill its dead for good.*"

— THE WORDS
JEAN-PAUL SARTRE

MY SISTER

MY SISTER! MY TEACHER! IN 1952, she had two weeks' advance knowledge of the theory and practice of the wasting disease. I want you to see her. She is my companion-in-arms.

No goddess, nor villain. A child of twenty-nine. Two years of college. Presented to society in late 1943. A woman of great sport and warmth.

She likes sailing, and tennis. She is a good swimmer, with a broad fine stroke in the school of the Australian Crawl. She loves cooking, and from time to time, I would hear her in the kitchen, humming tunelessly to herself.

Of all the unlikely people, of all the unlikely people to be kissed by the grey disease: who would have guessed? As of the second of September, she is laid in the hospital bed by poliomyelitis. By the sixth of September, they have laid her in an iron lung so that she can continue to breathe. And on the 29th of December, of the same year, they lay her in the grave.

She has never thought about the functioning of her body. She has no idea in the world how her various muscles combine in their workings with bone in a magic way to carry her through the range of motion: the complex interface of muscle and bone and nerves, the action and reaction of dendrons, axons, neurons, cytons that makes it possible for her to climb into a sailboat and spend a day racing before the wind on the St. Johns River. I am sure that the knowledge of how it is done never comes to her. Nor the importance of it. It never occurs to her. At least, not until late summer 1952.

She a *naif* who spends twenty-nine years of her life harming no-one and loving, to the depths she is able, a few close family members and a husband. She is an innocent, slightly freckled child who plays a fair game of tennis, and who trails her red hair behind her like a fire.

She contracts polio in late August and in the intense stage, it moves slowly over the entire field of her body. When the fever departs, she has one muscle remaining: in her left foot. Because of the loss of her breathing apparatus, she is fitted with a machine that breathes for her. "Whoosh" it goes, fifteen times a minute, nine hundred times an hour.

She cannot scratch her knee should it itch. She cannot bring food to her own mouth. She cannot brush back her fine red hair. She cannot wash nor wipe herself. She cannot reach out to hold another's hands.

In her respirator, she is flat on her back. She is turned every hour or so to prevent the development of bedsores that can become malignant and score the body down all the way to white bone. The regularity of the bellows punctuates her every moment, asleep or awake. "Whoosh." "Whoosh." A submarine: she is lying in a submarine. Warm. Protected. With light bulbs, festooning the iron lung, like a newly constructed building, or a Christmas tree. A submarine with portholes all along the side, so you can peer in and see where the muscles have disappeared from bone.

She, my sister, the originator and founder of all this pain, is now quite thin. Bones show beneath flesh, a picture out of Dachau. A woman's once graceful body now has knobby knees, knobby elbows, celery root. The hip bones jut up from a wasted stomach. The entire skeletal frame is pushing to get out, to get born, to be done with this painful flesh.

Her eyes are quite large now. Her face so shrunken and drawn that the eyes start out as if she were some night creature, startled in her submarine body. "Whoosh." She views you, the room, the world, upside down through a mirror. People stand outside her new breathing machine, up near the head, and wonder what to say. If they stand, she looks at their legs (legs that move!) If they sit, she sees their faces backwards. Friends' faces are turned around, turned obverse.

She who never thought seriously about sickness, nor her body, nor death, is thinking on them now, thinking hard on them. And she wonders what to say to the reversed faces of her old friends who cannot imagine *who cannot imagine* what it is like to be in the pale tan submarine, with all the dials and meters, and the bellows that go "whoosh" fifteen times a minute, nine hundred times an hour.

And if they talk, and they do talk, and if she replies, and she does reply, her words are turned wispy, hard-to-hear, for the talking mechanism is dependent on lungs and air, and her lungs have been deprived of power to push air and words.

And when she talks, and she talks so that you can barely hear her, she talks on the exhale, because she cannot talk on the inhale (one does not fight the submarine), which means that her sentences are interrupted fifteen times each minute, for the breathing machine to make her breathe, which makes conversations with her quite lei- surely, long pauses in the sentences, and everyone learns to be patient, very patient, with this new woman in her new submarine, who has become very patient.

Very, very patient. Doesn't demand too much, really. Can't demand too much. Except that you feed her when hungry (she is not very hungry) and bathe her when dirty (she is not very dirty, doesn't play in the mud too much) and dry off that place near the corners of her eyes when sad (she is sad very much because she doesn't know what has happened to her, nor why) and be with her when she thinks on the things that are gone now, like body and arms and legs and motion which are gone now, so soon now, things that she loved, gone so soon now, like sailing and tennis and running into the surf at the beach on the Atlantic Coast, and most of all, the ability, that important ability to scratch her knee, when it begins to itch, or turn over in her sleep, which she doesn't do very much any more, sleep that is, because of the noise, and confusion, and the strange change that has come over her body, which with the six nurses and orderlies and nurse's aides and the eight doctors and technicians and physical therapists, which with all these people working at her body, somehow doesn't seem to be her body any more at all, at all.

They give her a mirror, over her face, turned at a forty-five-degree angle, attached to the submarine, the submarine that pumps away, with its engine pumping away. They give her a mirror so that she can see the world, so she doesn't have to look at the ceiling, the light green institutional ceiling, with the flies, and the single naked light bulb. She is given a mirror, her own mirror, so that she can watch the world go by outside her door, there in her hospital room. She doesn't know if her room has a view out the window, because she isn't turned that way, but rather, turned so that she can see out into the hall, see the nurses and orderlies and doctors, who come in to do things to her

body, her new body, a body which has come up with such
new experiences of pain, of new pain. She never thought
she would be capable of surviving such pain. She never
thought she would, my sister didn't: but she did. For a
while, for a while.

They bring in a television set, into her room, and
she becomes a fan of baseball, watching baseball through
her mirror, on the new-fangled television set. She never
cared for baseball before, before all this happened. She
cared for sailing, and tennis, and some golf, from time to
time (she was very good at the long stroke, in the first,
fourth, and eighth holes at Timuquana Country Club), but
she never really cared for baseball, at least not until now, but
the afternoon nurse, Miss Butts, likes baseball, so they
watch it together, and my sister can watch the Dodgers
(whom she never heard of before) playing the Pirates
(whom she never heard of before) and she watches the
occasional home run in the mirror, when the batter hits the
ball, and takes off, and runs to third base, then to second,
then to first, and finally to home. It is comforting, in a
funny sort of way, to know that people still play, think of,
watch, write on, report on, worry about something like
baseball.

They never taught her very much about life, and the
body, and muscles and things, before this. When she was at
Stephens College, they taught her dance, and music, and a
smattering of literature courses, and some math, and a little
chemistry. But they never taught her about the catheter
stuck into her urinary tract, which stays there to drain the
piss that won't come out on its own, and how urine crystals
grow, so that when they pull the catheter out, it is like they
are ripping out the whole of her insides, her entire urethra

shredded, to ribbons, by these crystals, that come out of her, and no pain-killers, they give her no pain-killers, because this is a disease of the nervous system, and it might affect the regeneration of nerves. They taught her some math, and a little chemistry, and how to dance, at Stephens College, but they never taught her the new dimensions of pain, which she never ever thought she could bear, never, in a thousand years, but she does, she does, even though she never thought she could.

They taught her how to diagram sentences; and they taught her about Mozart, and Beethoven. They showed her the difference between the Samba and the Rumba, and between the Waltz and the Foxtrot, she remembers her teacher played "Besame Mucho" over and over again, so they could learn the Samba — but they never taught her about her lungs, the beautiful rich red alveoli that lose the ability to aspirate themselves, so that one night, they think she is clogging up, suffocating, and the doctor comes, with all the lights, and slices into the pink flesh, at the base of her neck, the blood jets up all over, and she can see the reflection of her neck in the mirror of his glasses, as he cuts into her neck (no anesthetics permitted because they affect the dark grey nerves nestled in the aitch of the spinal column, and polio got there first) the blood goes all over his smock, a drop of her blood even flecks his glasses, and of a sudden no air comes through nostrils or mouth, and she is sure she is suffocating, the very breath has been cut out of her, and her doctor punches a three inch silver tube down into her lungs, so that every two hours they can pump out the mucous, that collects in her lungs: they never taught her what it feels like to breathe through a little silver navel in her throat, never taught her about the feel of mucous being pumped from her lungs. They never taught her about the kiss of the trachea, the silver kiss, at the base of the neck, the kiss of this silver circle, the silver circle of the moon.

She was quite good at chemistry, my sister was: quite good. She got special honorable mention, at graduation, from Stephens College, there in Central Missouri. What she remembers most about Stephens is the spring evenings, when the smell of hay would drift into the classrooms, make her feel so alive, in the rich fecundity of Central Missouri, the rich hayfields, and the people moving so slowly, on a spring day, through the fields, those rich fields of hay. Or in the fall, when the moon would peer up over the fields come hush by midnight: the moon growing a silver medallion, hanging there in the sky, the sky so black, the moon so white-dust-silver. They gave her a silver medallion, for her chemistry, she was surprisingly good at it, not so good at literature, she never cared for Dickens, or Jane Austen, but she was so good at H_2SO_4, and $NaCl$, and MnO_2 that they gave her a special ribbon, with a silver moon on it, which she hung on her neck, which hung where the new silver moon of the tracheotomy hangs now, her badge, the badge of a job well done, a job well done, in the new education on the nature of the body, and its diseases, and the way the body will try to kill off its own, because of the diseases, and the deterioration of the kidney, bladder, lungs, heart, mind, under the sweet kiss of the disease, under the sweet new kiss of the disease.

My sister: the new student! The student of the body, and a student of disease, and perhaps even a student of sainthood: Sainthood. The questions of the nuns and priests and ministers of all religions of all times. If a tree falls in the forest, and no one is around, and no one hears it, was there really a sound? Or, can God create a rock, such a huge rock that He Himself cannot lift it? Or, can God create a disease, such a painful awful burning disease, of the nervous system, that invades the tender spinal chord, and scars the nerves therein so completely, with such pain and destruction of the self, that one can wish not to live any more? To live no more.

My sister. An innocent saint. For slightly less than four months, from 2 September 1952 to 29 December 1952, she will have ample time to work on her sainthood. She will have 2,832 hours to recall growing up in the sun of Florida, her shadow a black hole on the burning white sands of the beach.

I69,920 minutes: she will have almost a hundred and seventy thousand minutes to remember running for a fast lob on the white-line tennis courts at the Timuquana Country Club. She will have over ten million seconds, there in her new submarine, to remember that for twenty-nine years she had a constant companion, namely her body. A companion which asked little and gave much and, of a sudden, in the early fall of that year, turned a dead weight like a tree which has had the life leeched out of it. So dead, so weighted, that she must ask the good nurse to scratch her forehead, move a leg, adjust the hair, or brush away the wetness that forms of its own accord at the corner of her blue-gray eyes, just below those beautiful ruddy lashes, that match her beautiful ruddy skin — turning quite pale now.

The body ceases to function as a body, and commences to try to kill itself off. Bladder infection, kidney stones, phlegm accretion in the lungs, bedsores, respiratory dysfunction, depression. Over the next three months and twenty-seven days, my sister's body, the body which has been so kind all these years, will turn enemy and try to sabotage every machine (from within and without) which makes it possible for her to survive. Her body will attempt to murder her.

And shortly before dawn, nineteen hundred and fifty-two years after the Birth of Our Lord and Savior, two days before the end of that dark year, at 4:47 in the morning, in some anonymous respiration center in North Carolina, where she has been sent for reeducation of what is left of her body, in the company of some one hundred other machine-bound patients, just as the first of winter dawn is beginning to crack the still and snowy Chapel Hill sky, my sister will awaken for the last time to find her lungs clogged with the suppurating thickness of pneumonia.

There is to be a battle, a short one. A creature is squatting on her chest, trying to keep air from its proper place in her lungs. It is a silent and a lonely battle. There is no crying out. She is alone, and thinking "This is not happening to me," and for some unexplainable reason she remembers a spectacular day from last summer, with the sun coming down over the water, a spectacular day on the St. Johns River running before the wind in a White Star sailboat. She remembers the wind in her hair, and her body riding, riding on the swells from the great dark Atlantic near the jetties, and that great flowing expansive feeling of having all of life before her, of having the wind and the river and the freedom to ride them and be alive, so full of the freedom of being alive at the very edge of the river, just before it merges with the great wide dark deep Atlantic Ocean before her.

"This is not happening to me," she thinks. She cannot believe a termination of self and being in this huge room of clanking machines on a snow-dawn in North Carolina. "This is not happening to me," she thinks, but she is wrong. She is drowning in the liquids of her own body, and there is no way she can call out, to tell the nurse that she is suffering.

My sister! My sister. She is quite alone in her struggle as the sun begins to break through the grey waste outside. She tries to breathe in, cannot, and suddenly there is no spirit in her. My sister. Eyes, mouth, heart, single moving muscle in foot cease. There is no more warmth within or without, beyond the artificial heater placed inside the submarine which, as of now, has discharged its last patient.

The iron maiden continues to pump dead lungs for over an hour before the night nurse discovers the drowned creature, grey froth on blue lips. My sister, who never did anyone any harm, who only wished joy for those around her, now lies ice and bone, the good spirit fled from her.

— FROM *THE CRIPPLE LIBERATION FRONT MARCHING BAND BLUES*

THE BIBLE AND ZEN
By Pastor A. W. Allworthy

Moses says, "God — are you saying you want me to go back to the city and tell my friends that they have to leave their homes and march out into the desert? They'll think I'm some kind of a nut case. What am I supposed to say when they ask me where I'm getting these orders from?"

God says, "Look — tell 'em that your orders came from the God of their fathers."

Moses says, "Great — the God of their fathers. And they'll say 'Oy! The God of our fathers. Who's that?' What do I say then?"

"That's when you tell them, 'I AM THAT I AM.' They ask you who sent you and you just say 'I AM' sent you.

And Moses claps his hand to his forehead and says "!"

— EXODUS 3:14

T HE CHRISTIAN BIBLE IS ONE OF THE great artistic and social documents of the western world. Unfortunately, it has suffered two vicious attacks on its glory and its wisdom in the last few decades.

The first is that the original King James version has been rendered into a dozen or more "modernizations" that not only annihilate the poetry of the original, but — in the process — twist its messages to reflect whatever dogma is being pushed by the translator.

The second, and far more destructive, is that it has been arrogated by very those peculiar Americans called

Fundamentalists. The Baptists, Pentecostals, and Evangelicals claim to have inerrant knowledge of what it is supposed to be telling us. Because of them, the Bible has been turned into a new standard revised version of *Mein Kampf*, with our sweet dark and mysterious Jesus transmogrified into a tall, blue-eyed Atilla the Hun.

This perversion gives the Fundamentalists freedom to espouse the most appalling dicta under the banner of God's Own Truth. They claim, for example, that the Bible demands that women stay in the kitchen, that international wars are fit instruments for conveying the word of Christ, that capital punishment is not only permitted but desirable, that all gun control is *verboten*, that cancer patients are suffering and the disabled are in wheelchairs because they are sinners. It can be very dark in the hearts of those who claim they are Washed in the Blood of the Lamb.

The three most successful religions of the last century are Shintoism, Islam, and Christianity. It is no accident that they are also the most violent. Shintoism, a religion of ancestor worship, made it possible for Japan to conquer most of Asia and win a war against Russia in the early years of the 20th century. It was defeated only by a Christian Crusade mounted by America, England, and their colonies between 1941 and 1945. Islam — the religious faith of the Muslims — is just beginning to avenge the Christian Crusades of the 12th 13th, and 14th Centuries (they have never forgotten).[32] Their war against Christianity is oiled by their ownership of over sixty-five percent of the world's known oil reserves.

But the fundamentalists of Japan and the Middle East don't have a corner on doctrinal hate and violence. Those who have a need to find virulence in the Christian Bible can easily do so. There are the famous passages in Deuteronomy that advise parents of rebellious sons to have them stoned to death. Likewise, the parents of a daughter who is found not to be virgin can have "the men of her city" pelt her with rocks "that she die" (the man responsible for violating her is merely fined a hundred shekels.) Those who worship other gods shall be set upon "with stones, till they die."

Deuteronomy has specific restrictions against the disabled. A man who is "wounded in the stones [the testicles], or hath his privy member cut off, shall not enter into the congregation of the Lord." The book of Leviticus specifically states that the disabled cannot participate in religious services or practices: "A blind man, or a lame, or he that hath a flat nose, or anything superfluous... or a man that is broken footed, or brokenhanded, or crookbackt, or a dwarf, or that hath a blemish in his eye, or be scurvy, or scabbed, or hath his stones broken cannot take of the bread."

It was pretty mean back in Old Testament days, and those of our contemporaries who look to the Bible for

---

[32]One of the key tenets of Mohammedanism as expounded in the *Koran* is to offer an infidel a chance to become a convert to Islam. If he refuses, the Muslim may then safely cut the infidel's throat and the holy murderer will "rise straight to heaven." In addition, the *hudad* — the listing of criminal laws spelled out in the *Koran* — requires that fornication be punished by 100 strokes of a cane, and apostasy by crucifixion.

divine and unerring guidance can get pretty mean, too —
especially towards the disabled.

The task of the New Testament was to change all
this. Jesus was a member of the Essenes, a Jewish sect that
preached humility, poverty, and pacifism. He was a revolutionary, fighting the Old Testament dicta of gratuitous
cruelty. He told his followers to give up their riches, to give
up their hate against other religions and other peoples, to
be rid of their passion for violence. He was also a man of
love. (It is obvious that he was lover to at least one of his
apostles.[33] Two thousand years ago, homosexual love was
not considered to be strange or unusual. After all, Jesus was
living in the Roman Empire, which countenanced such
practices. It is only in our own time that those who fear for
their own manhood not only pervert the spirit of the love of
Jesus, but rise up to demand that the rest of us do it too.)

You can see why the Fundamentalists — despite all
their words to the contrary — loathe and despise the
Biblical Jesus, and do their damndest to translate him out
of existence. If He were alive today, they would be first in
line to pull out their 45's and pistol-whip Him for His
revolutionary messages and then look on passively as He
breathed His last in the gas chamber for His treasonous
statements.

The reason that we must deplore this kidnapping
and rape of Jesus and the Bible is that, in the process, some
of the more glorious parts of our heritage are lost. Jesus
spent at least a third of his life studying with the Buddhists

---

[33]"Now there was leaning on Jesus' bosom one of his disciples, whom Jesus
loved…" (John 13:23); "Lord, thou knowest all things; thou knowest that I love
thee…" (John 21:17).

of northern India.[34] There are hidden in the New Testament, as in the Old, a multitude of Tantric, Buddhistic, Taoist, Hindu, and Zen messages.[35]

Consider the quote from Exodus that appears at the beginning of this article. Moses wants to know God's name so he can introduce Him to his friends. And God tells him that His name is "I AM THAT I AM."

I-am-that-I-am. A statement directly out of Buddhism: paradoxical, saying everything and nothing, leaving us to contemplate the glorious contradictions that are as much the problem of our lives as our unstable reliance on words.

Or look at the passage in Exodus 33:20 - 23 that is stonily ignored by most of the contemporary religionists. They often translate this part of the Bible in such a way as to lose the lusty crudeness of it — because of their their unwillingness to acknowledge the earthy humor of our religious forebears, and the earthy nature of all of us.

---

[34]During his studies in India, Jesus was taught to achieve what the Yogis call *samadhi* — the ability to transcend the body, the ego, and the self through extended meditation. Thus, it is reasonable to speculate that He plunged Himself into a deep trance during the hours He was on the cross. Because of their ignorance of Buddhistic technique, His disciples confused this trance state with death — which, to the lay person, it resembles. It was only after being taken down and placed in the tomb that Jesus revived Himself and astounded His followers by appearing again before them. Not being aware of his *samadhi* training, and because of their superstition, they were convinced that He had died and been reincarnated. Jesus did nothing to disabuse them of this false assumption. Their ignorance of Eastern practices has thus created, over the centuries, a plethora of confusion about Jesus's final days with them. This confusion continues to plague Christianity even to this day.

[35]Some of the more famous koans to be found in the New Testament are "I see men as trees, walking..." (Mark 8:24); "Let the dead bury their dead..." (Matthew 8:22); "Strait is the gate..." (Ibid. 7:14); "We have piped unto you, and ye have not danced..." (Ibid. 11:17); and — perhaps the most famous of them all, being the last words of Jesus — "Feed my sheep" (repeated three times), and then, "Verily, verily, I say unto thee, When thou wast young, thou girdest thyself, and walkedst whither thou wouldest: but when thou shalt be old, thou shalt stretch forth thy hands, and another shall gird thee, and carry *thee* whither thou wouldest not." John immediately follows this with his own translation, assuming that it has to do with death and glorification — but most experts agree that the message is far different.

It's Moses again, demanding of his (and our) God:

"Let me look at You."

"No, you can't. You can't look at my face because there's no man that can look at me and live.

"But I have an idea [says God]: there is a rock near here, and you go stand up on it. As I'm passing, I'll set you up on the top of it, and I'll cover you with my hand as I go by, but then I'll take my hand away, and you can look at my ass, and that's it, Moses. Because there isn't anyone that can look on my face and survive."

⧗

It is not just "Exodus" or "Genesis" that bespeaks an Eastern view of God. The "Song of Solomon" tells of a passionate love affair between a white man and a black woman — both, apparently, unmarried — and it is as loving in its delicious passion as any of the eastern manuals on Tantric love.

Or there is the Book of Ezekiel, starting out with a perfect description of an ecstatic fantasy, drug- or god-induced:

And I looked, and, behold, a whirlwind came out of the north, a great cloud, and a fire infolding on itself, and a brightness was about it, and out of the midst thereof was the color of amber, out of the midst of the fire.

Also out of the midst thereof came the likeness of four living creatures. And this was their appearance: they had the likeness of a man.

*And every one had four faces, and every one
had four wings.*

*And their feet were straight feet; and the sole of
their feet was like the sole of a calf's foot: and they
sparkled like the color of burnished brass.*

*And they had the hands of a man under their
wings on their four sides, and the four had their faces
and their wings.*

⧗

There is, finally, the Book of Job, one of the true
glories of the Old Testament. It is a description of a good
man, one who follows all the commandments, who wakes
one day to find himself plagued with poverty, sickness, the
loss of his entire family, and — just to thicken the broth —
agonizing boils, from the crown of his head to the tips of his
toes.

"Why is God doing this to me?" Job asks his friends
Eliphaz, Bildad, and Zophar.

"You have sinned," they say.

"That's not true," says Job. "I've been a good man
and followed the commandments."

"You've sinned," says his friends.

"No," says Job — "something else is happening. I
am being punished for some other reason."

As it turns out, Job is right. He is being punished
not for his sins, but rather because the devil said to God one
day, "The only reason that Job is faithful to you is because
you've rewarded him. Take away his health, his family, his
riches, and he will curse you and revile you."

And God says, "OK, let's do it." And they take away Job's health, his family, and his riches.

And to the glory of his God, Job does not revile and deny Him, but continues to revere Him.

Which, I hasten to point out to you, is very Zen.

⧗

That there are millions of religionists in America who believe that the disabled are suffering because they have sinned. According to a recent *Los Angeles Times* poll, over forty percent of Christians believe that disease and sickness is "God's punishment for those who have sinned."[36] In other words, they see our God as a vengeful God intent on using his power to hurt and humiliate us. This is the very God that Jesus told us was no more.

The three friends of Job — Eliphaz, Bildad, and Zophar — come on to him as the Fundamentalists come on to the disabled. "You are suffering," they say, "because you have sinned."

---

[36]They're not the only ones. Many of the New Age folks believe that cancer patients, heart-attack victims, and the disabled bring their agony on themselves through an active but hidden need for self-destruction. One of the most astonishing examples of this can be found in *The Best of the Sun, Volume I,* available from *The Sun,* Chapel Hill, NC. The section entitled "Facing the Struggle" consists of a series of letters written by a psychotherapist named Peg Staley after discovering that she has breast-cancer. She describes searching back and forth across America for relief through non-traditional cures: NLP training, tai-chi, visspassana meditation, visualization therapy, Feldenkrais, enema therapy, psychosynthesis, psychic healing, Interface training, channeling, the "Dr. Kelley" diet — plus reading everything she can get her hands on.

It's a fascinating journey through late 20th Century American "healers" and "counselers." Unfortunately, there is a heavy dose of self-blame: "I began to suspect that I gave myself cancer to buy his [her husband's] love. To get sick to get attention is an old familiar pattern in our family." Further on, in one particularly cruel passage, she reports that her New Age counseler "worked with the deep unconscious part of me that is giving me cancer...that part which, having walled up, needed to break out of the cell and to live whatever the cost."

The evangelicals obviously have not read the book of Job with an open mind and an open heart, and for a very good reason: the message is that saintly, holy people suffer not from sin but from the intricacies of a relationship between the *worshipper* and *worshipped*. It has to be — by definition — a random, arbitrary relationship, subject to no sensible rules.

As I say, it is very Zen. Job suffers not because he is bad, but because God and the Devil have worked out a deal to test him and see if they can break him. No matter how ghastly it may sound, it's an excellent description of what man must expect if he chooses to worship a God who is outside himself.

The next time one of those inerrants comes up to tell you that you are disabled because you have sinned, suggest that he might spend some time studying his Bible. You might even point out to him that there is no sin except for the one that comes from separation from the universe and other humans. Since all of us are divine, such separation creates intolerable pain.

Once you begin to understand what is meant by this, you can begin to end it.

— EXCERPTED FROM THE INTRODUCTION TO
A BIBLE FOR THE 21ST CENTURY,
WITH TRANSLATIONS BY PASTOR A. W. ALLWORTHY.

A MEETING WITH MILTON ERICKSON

By Carlos Amantea

ONE OF MY JOURNEYS LED ME, SEVEN years ago, into the office of Milton Erickson. It was long after he had given up private practice, and, as it turned out, shortly before he died. He was spending four hours a day in "seminar." That's what they called them. That's not what they really were. These are the notes I made at the time:

Milton Erickson moved to Phoenix in 1949 for his health. He lives in a tract house on 12th Street, in a polyglot, hapless-looking part of the city. The meetings take place in a room that appears to be half kitchen, half living room. His wheelchair is crammed awkwardly through the doorway of the room where the ten us of are ranged. We are sitting on 1955 Motel Moderne furniture which I doubt has changed any in the last decade. Erickson wears his famous purple robes (he is color-blind — the only color he can see is bright purple). He also wears a purple shirt, and purple knit booties, all of which make him look like a giant baby.

There are desert artifacts everywhere: skulls, stones, desert bird bones. The air conditioner (it is June) is noisy, and inefficient and cranky; and the traffic outside on 12th Street is just as noisy.

The doctor sits in his uncomfortable wheelchair — no footrests — on a giant foam cushion, his bootied feet scarcely touching the purple carpet on the floor. He had polio twice: once in 1917 and again during the last great epidemic of the early fifties. He has no use of his right hand and little of his left. His one motion is to lean forward awkwardly to observe the visitors, or to sit back uncomfortably, in his chair. He looks like a great stuffed panda with huge, glaucous, penetrating eyes.

He gives "audiences" — my words, not his own — six days a week to psychiatrists, psychologists, M.D.s, psychiatric social workers, and counselors who come from all over the continent to spend four hours in this room, listening to him — listening to him "tell stories."

It is hot and close in the room. Often, it is impossible to hear what he is saying. Not only do the traffic and air conditioner create too much ambient background noise, but polio has robbed Erickson of many of the muscles of throat, mouth, tongue, and lips. His words are difficult to hear, and often, he will go into coughing spasms — wheezing with great, weak indraughts of breath — so he sounds not unlike one on his death-bed. "Just my luck," I think. "I spend months angling to see him, and he dies on the first of the days I'm to be here." Since my coughs often sound the same, I have the cold comfort of imagining us going together into the mesmeric hereafter from this dingy, no-exit room.

This is the master. It is an honor to be here. Thousands try, few get past the eagle eyes of his wife, who is also the reservations secretary. This is some feudal court out of the Ch'in Dynasty, and only the select out of the masses get to the court (some court!) of the wise man.

A whole industry has risen about visiting the Prophet of Phoenix. One comes for a day or two, and then advertises that one has "studied under Milton Erickson." This means you can charge, $1,000 a day for seminars. Few pay attention to the fact that the master himself charges only $25 a day for visitors. I think I love him for that reason if for no other. He doesn't care about money, getting rich, making it in the American dream factory. He gives away information, knowledge, insights — gives them to all comers for so little.

His stories are Zen koans which follow each other without pause. Many of them are familiar. We have already read them in "Psychology Today," or in the many articles he has authored himself, or in one of the many books about him by Jay Haley, Ernest Rossi, Jeff Zeig, or Bandler and Grindler (two California heavies who are the Rosencrantz and Guildenstern of the Ericksonian movement). There are also dozens of videotapes floating around of hypnotic sessions, where you can watch him put people in trance and they sit there unmoving, one hand frozen halfway between knee and face, and he mutters incomprehensible things to them, and they nod and smile or weep a little bit, and he mutters again, and they sit there motionless. These tapes are treasured by the followers of Erickson, but to some of us they are more like a weekend festival of repeated showings of *Last Year at Marienbad* alternating with Andy Warhol's eight-hour-long documentary footage of the Empire State Building.

Many who come to the sessions already know the punchlines of the stories he tells. But there is a difference in hearing them directly from his lips. His voice is so quiet, his lung power so shot with post-polio syndrome (a gradual weakening of the remaining muscles, decades after the original onslaught of the disease) that whole words, or sentences are sometimes lost in the babble of street noises and moving about the room.

No matter — half the audience seems to be in hypnotic trance. As Erickson speaks, he plays us like some great chromatic organ, putting this or that person into trance, keying words to one or another of us. And the whole thing is so subtle that I sometimes think nothing at all is happening. At other times, I am dead sure that this giant purple panda knows everything going on in the room, and is making some magic music with our minds and psyches, testing our *aqua vitae*, checking to see if our mental pumps are working, adjusting screws here and nuts there, then plunging with us into the pool of our souls, to come up with bits and pieces of our gossamer selves that don't necessarily belong in this dusty, stifling room in Phoenix, Arizona on one of the hottest days of June, 1979.

The stories ramble on in apparent random order. There is the one of the two nurses who think their husbands are "sexually perverted." There is another of the nurse who was required to squat over a mirror, so that she could learn to have intercourse. Her husband was required to learn how to masturbate, "to get an erection at will, and that's no man named Will." His stories use puns, and anagrams, and poetic techniques right out of Shakespeare, and are often just as obscure. Sometimes I catch myself thinking, "What am I doing here, listening to this nonsense?" This old man, an old man with glittering eyes — not unlike the eyes of some of the more frightening desert snakes. "I flew to Phoenix for this?" I think. "What would it be like if nothing were happening — nothing at all? Suppose we are so sucked in by his myth that we will believe anything?" I remember what I once read about people who were always trying to analyze his stories for some secret meaning. He called them "city slickers."

I am sweating on my Drugstore-Cowboy Nauga-hyde Chair, and there is a long confusing story about a man with claustrophobia whom Erickson put in a closet, and he closes the door one millimeter, and the wall behind him, and he closes and opens the door, and closes the door, and opens it, and closes the door, and closes the door, and each time he says "close," I find my eyes closing, and I can not and do not wish to open them. I am in one of the famous Ericksonian trances and want to stay there as my mind struggles with trying to remember all his articles about telling stories with all those trance-inducing words in them, and of overcoming people's resistance to being put under. One of the ladies in the audience — sobbing — has found some secret grief in the story he is telling, a sadness stuck in it, clove-in-the-onion style, touching her in her deep trance. "She's getting something and I'm not," I think jealously; "I want it too." I remember when I forced myself to drag through two sequential weekends of *est*, so I could get It — and I remember not getting It, and thinking "What's wrong with me? Why can't I get It?"

At the break, I go into the bathroom, and steal some of the Ericksonian Aim for my breath, so I won't offend my seatmates when I go into the Ultimate Trance. I come back and stand about, trying to avoid that butt-breaking Nauga-hyde chair, and I am sort of dreaming, and I look at Erickson, at his eyes, so heavy-lidded, and they widen — all pupil, no iris, as he shoots a visual arrow at me, then down at the chair, a look that says "Siddown Buster!" and I do, with alacrity. Does he have that power because we all acknowledge that he is the master? Or is he the master because he has all that power?

Later, we visit his house next door. His coach-dog growls at me. There are purple gowns and white orthopedic corsets hanging on the clothesline. He has a purple telephone, and he writes in purple. Three of the seven in audience today wore purple in homage to him. He shows us photographs of children and grandchildren. I wonder what it would be like to grow up the child of Milton Erickson. He was probably one of the first professionals to propound the idea known by all good mothers that, as a parent, you never violate the experience of your child. He told Jay Haley about his son at age five, taking a bad fall down the back stairs. Between the boy's screams, Erickson would say "That hurts awful, Robert, and it will keep right on hurting." He was confirming the child's feelings, instead of doing what so many parents do, those that say, "Oh, pooh — that doesn't hurt at all," confusing the child about what is being felt, against what some authority-parent says about what should be felt.

⌛

The Erickson house is filled with ironwood statues of dogs, octopuses, trees, ferns. My back hurts and so does my behind. I wish I could borrow a quick trance from him, have him tell me that it doesn't really hurt. What is it my friend Lorna says? — that Erickson spends three hours each morning reframing himself in trance, because of his painful arthritis. I would probably be just as well off back at the hotel in the jacuzzi, breathing the air that makes me sweat so copiously in this hundred-and-ten-degree city which, I am beginning to think, doesn't belong here at all.

Cathy and Lorna have traveled here with me from California. They are real therapists, and are the ones who got me in the door. After we leave Erickson's, we go to the bar in the Arizona Biltmore. They tell me some stories about him. Like most fans, they have a good complement of them gathered over the years, some of which are unpublished. We settle into a booth near the door. There is a live chamber group playing "Just a Violet." At the bar, a young man with a camera challenges a man in tie and jacket to a fight. Seems cameraman thinks the other man was making goo-goo eyes at his girlfriend, or wife, or hooker.

"Oh no," I say. They go out into the hall, right next to where I am drinking my Molsons, and the cameraman kicks the feet out from under the well-dressed fellow, and continues kicking him in the ribs, the back, the head, the face. "This is not happening," I think. "I'm still in a trance, aren't I?" I am in the elegant bar of the Frank Lloyd Wright designed Arizona Biltmore. There are ladies in long dresses, men in ties and formal jackets, waiters in tuxedos, and this American, macho brawl is happening right next to us out in the hallway. "Did you see how that woman played those two guys," says Cathy to Lorna, "played them just like a violin. Boy, you sure are scared," she says to me.

After the blood stops flowing and I come up from under the booth, I tell them about the old geezer who got into the hotel Jacuzzi with me this morning. This was the dialogue we had:

He: What happened to you?
Me: Polio.
He: When?
Me: Oh, twenty-five years ago.
He: You were born a cripple?

Me: No. I got polio twenty-five years ago. I ain't no spring chicken, you know.

He: What happened to you?

Me: What do you mean?

He: Didja have an auto accident?

Me: {RESIGNS}.

Lorna and Cathy talk more about Erickson. Lorna, on her tenth visit to see him, says that he is somewhat Nineteenth Century in his attitude towards women. He has many stories about women who revolt, become independent — but who ultimately come back to marry, raise a family, be happy. He says they find "the cradle of the womb" — that is, the blessings of motherhood. Later, she sends me an article called "Myths About Erickson" by Corydon Hammond of the University of Utah. It demonstrates that Erickson was a more careful, practiced technician than most people realize. It also shows that what people perceived as "tricks" were more in the nature of common sense. It contains the following dialogue between Erickson and "one brave student:"

"Were you directing that story to someone in the group for whom you sensed it was relevant?"

"No."

"Were there several of us that you felt needed to examine something illustrated in the story?"

"No"

"Were you hoping to fixate our attention as an indirect induction?"

"No."

"Well, was it a metaphor meant to convey something at unconscious levels?"

"No."

"Well, then, why did you tell the story?"

Erickson smiled. "I just thought it was an interesting story about good therapy"

That night I dream about long branches, a swamp, and two women talking about "pokeweed" — the plant with juicy berries that are used for making purple dye. There is a couch made of it. It is a hot, gulf night, heavy with an incipient storm. The couch is made of the same purple cloth as Erickson's clothes. The women are talking about being "three legged." There are swamp shadows, all about us, a hot storm coming.

I wake up at three or so burning with the dry Arizona air. I want a drink of water — badly — but not wanting it enough to go to the trouble of getting up, I lie there, with my mouth like chambray, thinking about water, and the hot desert, and storms: pokeweed, three-legged women.

At Erickson's the next day, Cathy and Lorna get me into the hot seat next to him. He is brought into the room, and before he can begin speaking, we pause for the ritual ceremony of the hooking up of the recorders: a spider's web of microphones and wires from cassette machines are attached to his purple robe. Most of the participants want to be sure that Erickson, and his words, don't escape them, forever. And recorders popping to a halt throughout the day don't seem to bother the master — just me.

We have something even more irksome than noisy tape recorders: a lady psychologist from New York. She is quite sizable, as is her voice. Like the rest of us, she can't understand half of what Erickson is saying, but instead of viewing this as The Breaks when you are around the master, she keeps interrupting him with "I didn't catch that," or "Whudja say, Doctor Erickson?" or "He put it up against her *what?*"

Erickson overlooks her strident interruptions for about an hour — he is remarkably patient; but then after she says, "I didn't hear, Doctor, they looked up into her what?" yet again — he gives her the *what*: He looks directly at her, closes his eyes, and, by my troth! — she falls back on the couch in a deep trance, staying there (where she well belongs) for a half hour or so. Then, as she bestirs herself, shaking her head and blinking, he looks at her wide-eyed again, closes his eyes, and again she falls back in a swoon where, I would guess, her hearing, insight, and peacefulness are considerably improved.

Erickson, as usual, asks for questions, and I say, "Yes, how do you put someone in a trance who doesn't want to go into a trance, and, number two, how do you treat headaches?" I tell him about the migraines I've had for the past thirty years.

He starts another series of stories: about a guy in the Wisconsin prison system who was a five-time loser; and then one about Sam, the alcoholic, who needed a place to stay, and so Erickson said he could stay in his backyard but he would have to give up his boots. The stories go on all day, and watching him, I think about how amazing he is. He has people from all over the world vying to spend a day with him. He is the acknowledged master of Reframing and Hypnotherapy. Under most circumstances, this old man would be put away in some home for the aged and crippled, but he has a force that has carried him on his own for seventy-five years, and he is still going strong: they say he only recently gave up his Sunday sessions. "I've been living on borrowed time for forty-five years," he's fond of saying, "and I don't have to pay it back"

He has carved out a therapy system all by himself, from himself, and has taught himself to work with all types: depressives, manic-depressives, schizophrenics, juvenile delinquents, suicides, and families (he is considered to be one of the earliest, and most original, practitioners of Family Therapy). He has mastered some of the most diverse methods of establishing rapport with patients. He has found, for one, that he could work with autistics by breathing in rhythm with them. He connects with patients by speaking their language. Someone will say things like "How does that grab you?" or "It was a real gut-wrenching experience." He has learned to spot this type of individual, and respond in kind: "Can you get a handle on what I'm saying?"

He learned to communicate with patients in what they call "the back wards" of mental hospitals by accepting their antisocial behaviors, and then redesigning them — on their terms — so that the cycle of depression, lunacy, or simple non-communication could be broken. He is one of the few to communicate successfully with schizophrenics who speak word salad (what Jung called "klang" speech). His method is to repeat the gibberish back to the patient changing only the vowels. It is said that after a while patients can't stand it any more, and will do anything to shut him up — even putting an end to their psychotic behavior patterns. There's only room for one in that crowded hotel of delusion.

At 2:45 he turns to me, and says, "Do you understand?"

"I don't know," I say.

"When did you know that you were going to ask me those two questions?"

"This morning, in the hotel, about ten."

"When did *I* know you were going to ask me those two questions?"

"I don't know," I say.

"When I saw you sitting in that chair," he says. "Close your eyes," he says. He makes a ring of thumb and forefinger with his one good hand, puts it about my wrist, raises my arm, and I am gone.

Now don't ask me what happened. I wasn't there, remember? I do recall a voice coming at me, and my hand moving up towards my face, stopping when it got to the halfway mark. I remember him whispering to me about pain, about taking a cool drink, and lying out in the sun. Then I hear him talk about "the devil looking over your shoulder," and have a powerful vision of a big fat gargoyle from some medieval French cathedral — a monster all lips and tongue, hovering there in front of my face, looking right at me.[37]

---

[37]The day of my trance, when we were driving back to the hotel, Lorna told us a story about Erickson. A farm worker, a Hispanic woman, had come to him in a state of profound depression because of her job. He prescribed electroshock therapy to cure her depression. "But," said Lorna, "Erickson being Erickson, before he would subject her to shock treatment, he perscribed it for himself. In that way, he knew first hand what it did to someone's psyche."

We all marvelled at the outrageousness of his using something as crude as shock treatments on a patient, but, at the same time, we acknowledged that he did it with typical Ericksonian flair. That night, I wrote up the story in my journal.

When I prepared the earliest drafts of *The Lourdes of Arizona*, I sent copies of it to several of the people I had gotten to know at the conference, including Lorna. She wanted to know where the hell I had gotten the "electro-shock *campesina* story." She claimed that she had never told me such a wild tale. Jeff Zeig, of the

When I come to, he and all the others are back in his office. He's signing their books and asking each lady for a kiss on the cheek. I stagger up, go to the bathroom for some more Aim, and there, right next to the sink, is a black spider. I turn on the light; I look closely and sure enough, there are those red triangles on the spider's belly or abdomen or whatever you call it. I go out to his office and announce, "There's a black widow spider in the bathroom and I was scared he was going to bite me." Lorna corrects me: "You thought she was going to bite you." Erickson goes on signing books.

Cathy, Lorna and I fly back to California that night. The next morning I developed the most wretched pain in my back, right under the shoulder blade. It stays there a full

Erickson Institute, who know Erickson and most of his stories, said that as far as he knew, Erickson had never prescribed electroshock for anyone, ever.

It took me a couple of years to figure it out. What I was dealing with was one of those famous Ericksonian "brain implants."

When I was in trance, Erickson left behind a post-hypnotic suggestion. In it, he told me to *create* a story with him in it. That story would tell me something very significant about me, and about me and him. "It will both please and surprise you" is the way he would phrase it.

We Crips trust very few people. We don't think anyone can understand the enormity of what has happened to us, and what happens to us each day of our lives. We commonly distrust doctors, strangers — even, at times, family and friends. We certainly distrust someone we were meeting for the first time — even another Crip.

Erickson wanted to be damn sure that I got his message. Therefore, he had me build a fictive story that would weave him into my world. The tale of the Spanish-speaking laborer forced into electroshock therapy contained language and symbols that I could comprehend in the deepest part of me. It was a tale I could fathom far better than the truth of my own state, which some part of me refused and still refuses to recognize.

I was a mythic foreigner, a strange woman in an unforgiving place, depressed with her lot, forced to go through shock under doctor's supervision. This was me in 1952. Twenty-five years later, a doctor who had followed the same route said to me, "You and I have been there together. You've been shocked — as was I. But there is a way out."

With this trance-induced message, he created a space inside me where before there had been nothing but shock and pain. In that space, I was given permission — by him, by me — to create a fable that not only fit into that space, but to begin the process of shaping, and healing, what had been there before.

And now, more than a decade after that, the permission, the healing, continues, and continues — as Erickson so often said — "to please and surprise me."

month. I can scarcely get out of bed for the first week. It wakes me at night, makes my days a misery.

I didn't have any headaches, though — for the first time in thirty years, I didn't have a single headache. Not for a full month. "How in God's name did he do that?" I wondered. "What did he say to me when he had me in that trance?"

He never gave me the opportunity to come back and question him about it. The old pokeweed son-of-a-bitch died a year or so later, a week before we were to go back for another visit.

— FROM *THE LOURDES OF ARIZONA*

VI. A NOTE
ABOUT THE AUTHOR

Once a week I spent a day in bed. I can remember looking at

my body with loathing and thinking, Boy, if I ever get to

heaven, I'm not going to ask for a new pair of legs like the

average quad does. I'm going to ask for a dick I can feel.

DON'T WORRY, HE WON'T GET FAR ON FOOT
JOHN CALLAHAN

THERE IS A FINE WINTER HEAT THERE where I live near the equator — ninety degrees in the shade during the day, seventy in the moon-shade at night. I have found to it be so pleasant for my old bones that I've been going south for several years now.

It was just recently that I met Jesús. No, no — not *that* one (that comes later). No, I'm talking about Jesús Esteban Rodriguez, my *mozo*. I needed someone to help me and to help me clean up my house — the house with no running water, no electricity, and plenty of dust. So I sent the word out, and I'm sitting alone on the patio one night, nursing my Anis Chinchón, listening to the waves, that eternal note of sadness coming in, and suddenly there's a voice out of the dark, saying, *"Se dice que necesita ayuda."*

He moved into the light of the candle, dark out of the dark and he's still dark: skin out of the cocoa-colored rivers of Oaxaca. Jesús with the solemn mouth, high cheek-bones, thick black hair to the shoulders, eyes direct. *"Se dice que necesita ayuda."* Not "I need work." Rather, "They say you need help."

Jesús has been with me on and off for the five years since that first meeting. He works, and works well — but he always preserves his independence, as befits the heir of those who grew up so many years under the thumbs of so many colonialists. He's independent without throwing it in my face. He also had something very important to teach me about CripZen.

It all took place last winter. It was one of the days I had chosen to go to the public market in the nearby town of Puerto Perdido. I wanted to buy some fish, and some tortillas, and some beer. When we got there I told Jesús to get my wheelchair out of the back of the car so we could go into the market. He said "No, it's all right, I'll just go in and get what we need." I said, "No, I want to go in." He said it would be easier if he did it all. And I thought to myself, you can defy me on almost anything else, Jesús, but when I want my wheelchair — I want it, and I want it *now*.

So I got out — slowly, by myself — and made my way (or rather, hunkered) around the car. It was hell on my shoulders, and it took forever because I had to cling to the rack atop the car so I wouldn't fall, my arthritis killing me all the while. I wanted to be sure that son-of-a-bitch saw what happened when he defied me. Crip Vengeance.

I got to the side door, and opened it, and tried to yank my wheelchair out, where — of course — it fell over on its side, still folded, into the dust. At this point (Jesús was watching this circus act out of the corner of his eyes), he got out, and lifted it up and opened it so I could sit in it. He said nothing.

He said nothing while we are shopping, and after we get back to the car, and when we get home. He said nothing to me for a long while, making himself busy elsewhere.

Finally, I tracked him down in the back garden, next to the Poperin Pear tree, and I said in my I-will-patiently-explain-it voice *"Mira, Jesús."* Look, Jesús. *"Estuve en hospital…"* You have to understand where I am coming from. I was in the hospital for two years. It took me another year to be able to get out of the house. I like going out in the world. I can't stand feeling caged up. I don't want to go to the public market just to buy things. I want to go because forty years ago I got stuck in places I didn't want to be stuck in, and I couldn't get out. That's why I wanted to go to the market today and not just sit in the car waiting for you to buy things for me.

Jesús' eyes (which are normally large, and lugubrious) narrowed a bit. He stood before me, every bit the fighter, rocking back and forth on the soles of his feet, narrow-eyeing me. He began to speak. His voice was unsure (he's a few decades younger than I) but he spoke straight on, uneasy but not afraid *he isn't afraid of me — he doesn't have any fear of what I am, what happened to me, what I think it did to me.*

"*No me importa,*" he said. I don't care. I don't care about the hospital, and how long you were there, and how long you were in a bed. It's not my problem. I don't care about all that. "*No me toca.*"

My history — so important to me, so big, so vital, so key — all that history to Jesús, "*no me toca, Lorenzo*" — it doesn't touch me, Lorenzo.

History, his-story. It's yours, not mine. "*No me importa.*" Here and now, that's where we are, he says. Don't give me any of that fuckin' his-story.

The Zen lesson of the day, of the year, of all time. It's your story, not mine. I will help you, care for you — perhaps even love you. But your troubles: they aren't my troubles. "*No me toca.*"

⧗

My friend Anna runs a school nearby, in Cipolete. There are some sixty age five-to-fifteen young Crips she's taken off the streets of the villages near there, got them out of their houses (some of them spent their childhoods chained to their beds). She puts them together in a place where they can learn to live with their bodies. They eat well, for the first time in their lives, and they make friends, and have medical help if they need it, and physical therapy, and braces and wheelchairs: all that they need to become mobile and alive and part of the world again.

Anna and I have gotten to know each other over the years, since I first started visiting the school, bringing down a few things to help keep it going. Since she is a non-Crip, I try to guess what her brood is thinking about, and I communicate it to her, as best I am able.

"All of us are angry," I tell her. "We may never say it, but what we really think is, 'You — The Normals — you don't understand. You'll never know what it's like.' This gives us the opportunity of sneering at you. It's a form of reverse discrimination."

Carlos, one of the patients there, moved around on his ass his whole life because he was club-foot. But recently, after the third operation in Oaxaca, he was able to get up on his feet. Anna saw him walking for the first time, across the campus, and she jumped up, and got everyone to cheer, loudly. Carlos scowled and went off and hid. She didn't understand why. "He seemed so angry," she told me.

"It was better if you didn't cheer him," I explained to her. Carlos at age seventeen wants nothing more than to be invisible (after all these years of being noticed — sometimes with excessive pity by the visitors there). "By cheering him, by singling him out," I told her, "even though it was a moment of tear-making triumph — you made him feel ashamed. Now that he can walk, he wants badly to leave his differentness behind. He wants people *not* to notice him." Sometimes, as I say, it is difficult for people to understand the weird twists and turns of the average CripMind.

In our continuing dialogue, as with all good compadres, Anna and I don't just talk about what's happening to us, and to the world around us. We talk about everything in the universe, up to but not excluding the meaning of life, the meaning of death, and — a subject we both relish — reincarnation. Anna claims she wants to come back as an ocelot, and as I look at her, she sitting there, smiling at me, her hair pulled back just so, with her calm and her contained power, I say, "I think you don't have to do a thing. I think you're already there.

"Me?" I say: "I want to come back as a penguin. Stomping about, diving in the cool waters, built-in tuxedo." But then, I think, if she comes back as an ocelot, and me as a penguin, how can we ever meet in the shade like this, to talk as we do, to laugh together.

I couldn't stop thinking about it afterwards. This thing about returning. I thought about her sidling through the woods, and me diving off glaciers, into the icy waters. Is there a place off Tierra del Fuego where ocelots and penguins meet for tea and crumpets?

"I don't mind if you come back as an ocelot, as long as we can meet from time to time," I wrote her, after I returned home. "But I have to tell you that I was lying about wanting to be a penguin. I can't stand ice, except in the glass of white wine that I have with dinner with my pills.

"I really don't care what they give me for a body, as long as they don't make me come back as me any more," I said. "You know I like myself well enough, have had fairly good times with me (some bad times, too).

"I've gained a certain respect for my taste in food and liquor and people, but I would still like to have the chance to work out with someone else's body for a change. Jane Fonda's, say. Bruce Springsteen's. Madonna's. Or the dusky, sunny fisher-lad we saw when we were there at the fruit-juice bar, in Puerto Perdido. You remember him, the one with the great sloe eyes, and the body like chocolate glacé, and the great quadriceps. (I certainly remember him, even if you don't).

"If they want me to come back with any real enthusiasm they'll have to stuff me into a body like that: a body a bit more serviceable than the one they gave me this last time around. I'm not all that picky, mind you, but I simply refuse to come back as a Crip gringo anymore, with all that dysfunctional plumbing, arms and legs that don't work worth shit, ridiculous aches and pains that take up too much of my days and nights.

" 'I've done that one,' I'll tell them. 'You want me to be divine don't you? Well, give me something nice to be divine in for a change.' "

If they give me a handsome new chassis, with quality fittings and a Deluxe polish-job, I'll do anything they want: make the prayers, light the candles, pay homage to the gods, put goldleaf on the divine's great toes. I'll be their slave.

Early on — after a few trial years — I'll even abandon any and all interest in sex, money-making, fighting the world, and all those causes that have taken too much of my time this time around.

"I'll be good, I promise you," I'll tell them. "I'll give up everything when I get through with the usual teen-age indiscretions. After just a few short years, I'll become a holy man, a wandering saddhu. I promise faithfully: I'll spend the rest of my years cheerfully walking the land, delivering Lordly messages, eating bark and drinking nothing stronger than leaf tea and branchwater, pausing only briefly near the beaches to look (only briefly, mind you!) at the figure I once was, the one I once wanted to be.

"I am sure that after they hear my plea," I tell her, "they'll be more than willing to trust me with a new, powerful, lithe body — so I can have some fun for the first few years of my new return, before I turn into the saint they (and all of us) can be so proud of."

BIOGRAPHICAL DATA

Pastor A. W. Allworthy was born in Diboll, Texas in August 1933. He was educated at the Fielding Bible School in Pharr, Texas, where he was awarded his DDD. He has preached extensively in both as a layperson and a scholar. He is the author of *The Petition Against God* (published by Christ The Light Works). It is a study of RM-2493, the infamous petition for rulemaking that was filed with the Federal Communications Commission in 1974 and has so far brought in over 30,000,000 letters of protest. Pastor Allworthy is also the author and translator of *A Bible for the 21st Century* to be issued in five or more volumes over the next decade by the same publisher. He lives in Richardson, Texas and has several children.

⧗

The late *Carlos A. Amantea* was born in Savannah, Georgia and was educated in psychology at Harvard and the Sorbonne. He lived much of his life in San Lorenzo, Honduras. His major life's work, *The Lourdes of Arizona*, has been published in English by Mho & Mho Works, and, in Spanish, by Cuatros Vientos of Santiago.

⧗

L. W. Milam was born in Jacksonville, Florida and studied English at Yale University, Haverford College, and the University of California at Berkeley. In the 60s and 70s, he started several non-commercial community broadcast stations, including KRAB in Seattle, KBOO, Portland,

KPOO, San Francisco, and KTAO, Los Gatos. He wrote a regular column for the Seattle *Post-Intelligencer* and has published articles in the Washington *Post*, the St. Louis *Post-Dispatch*, the San Francisco *Chronicle*, the Los Angeles *Times*, and the Vancouver *Sun*, among others. For several years, he was publisher of the book review magazine, *The Fessenden Review*. He has written several books on media, travel, family therapy, and disability. His book on starting a radio station for the community, *Sex and Broadcasting*, was widely cited as the seminal book on do-it-yourself media. The *Times Literary Supplement* called his most recent, *The Blob That Ate Oaxaca and Other Travel Tales*, "tenderly erotic."

He lives in California and thinks he is a dinosaur, lurking about in swampy areas late at night and eating water lilies.

NOTE

Today — which may be yesterday to you now, but can only be tomorrow for us yesterday (and vice-versa) — we learned that *Spinal Network* changed its name to *New Mobility*. No, matter — it's a good, no-nonsense magazine: free of cant, saccharin and fake triumph. You can and should subscribe to it. Six issues a year for $18 from Box 4162, Boulder, Colorado 80306.

This book was set in Goody Alphabetica, a fine, soup-like typestyle developed by Maurice Goody, brother to Sam, who ran the Broadway Deli down on West Third. The pages were originally printed on organic marzipan using biodegradable ink with a peanut-butter base, but they all got eaten so it was reformulated using a pure acid (LSD) infused paper. Thus, you might want to eat them after reading because of the vision thing.

The book was designed and typeset by Lauren Langford who thinks she's a lark. The cover, on the other hand, was designed by Lola Lark who thinks she's a wren.

Dear Mho & Mho Works:

Please send — postpaid —

☐ _____ copies of *The Cripple Liberation Front Marching Band Blues* by Lorenzo W. Milam at $9.95 each [orders for two or more copies — up to a maximum of five copies — will be entitled to a 20% discount];

☐ _____ additional copies of *CripZen* at $12.95 each [orders for two or more copies — up to a maximum of five copies — will be entitled to a 10% discount];

☐ _____ copies of *The Lourdes of Arizona* by Carlos Amantea for ☐$17.95 (hardcover) or ☐$10.95 (softcover) [orders for two or more copies — up to a maximum of five copies — will be entitled to a 20% discount];

☐ _____ copies of *The Petition Against God* by Pastor A. W. Allworthy for $3.95;

☐ _____ One each of *The Cripple Liberation Front, The Lourdes,* and *The Petition* for a special combined discount price of $19.95.

Name: _____

Address: _____

City/State: _____ Zip: _____

Please mail your order with check to:
Mho & Mho Works
Box 33135
San Diego CA 92163

California residents add 7.75% sales tax.

Sorry, we cannot honor credit card orders at these prices. If you want to order at the regular price with your MasterCard, VISA, Discover, or American Express, please call our order number: (800) 874-4688.